Limit of Liability/Disclaimer of Warranty

Neither we nor any third parties provide any warranty or guarantee as to the accuracy, timeliness, performance, completeness or suitability of the information and materials found or offered in this study guide for any particular purpose. You acknowledge that such information and materials may contain inaccuracies or errors and we expressly exclude liability for any such inaccuracies or errors to the fullest extent permitted by law.

Pharmacology for Technicians

Pharmacokinetics is the study of drug absorption, distribution, metabolism, and excretion (**ADME**). ADME can be affected by factors such as age, race, gender, genetics, dosage form, disease conditions, foods, and simultaneous usage of other drugs.

Drug absorption is the transfer of drugs into the bloodstream. Majors factors that affect drug absorption, especially when drugs are taken orally, include gastric emptying time, bile salts and enzymes, and intestinal movement. Gastric emptying time is affected by the amount and type of food in the stomach, other drugs, emotional state, and body position. The longer a drug stays in the stomach, the more likely it will be destroyed by stomach acids instead of being released into the bloodstream. Slow intestinal movement will result in greater drug absorption since the drug will be in contact with the intestinal membrane longer. Bile salts in the intestinal tract increase absorption of hydrophilic drugs; enzymes can destroy drugs and reduce absorption. The **half-life** of a drug is the amount of time it takes for the blood concentration of a drug to reduce by half.

Drug distribution is the transfer of drugs between the bloodstream and various body tissues/membranes. Drug distribution is affected by blood flow rates, tissue membrane permeability, and protein bindings. Drugs are distributed quicker to organs with high flow rates. Organs with high flow rates include hearts, liver, etc.; organs with low flow rates include muscle, skin, etc. Most tissue membranes are highly permeable; however, one membrane that is not easily permeable is the blood-brain barrier. Some drugs may bind to the proteins in blood plasma, preventing the drug from passing through the tissue membrane.

Drug metabolism, which primarily occurs in the liver, is the breakdown of drugs into compounds that can be excreted. As drugs are metabolized, the drug's therapeutic effects are reduced. Different people metabolize drugs at different rates and may require different doses to achieve the same therapeutic effects; those with higher metabolic rates would need higher doses. When a patient takes a drug chronically, the liver may increase its enzyme activity; this is called enzyme induction. Enzyme induction results in greater metabolism of a drug, so the patient will need to increase the dose of the drug to get the same therapeutic effects. Enzyme inhibition reduces enzyme activity and reduces metabolism of a drug.

Drug excretion, which primarily occurs through the kidneys, is the process by which drugs are expelled from the body. An impaired kidney or the use of other drugs that prevent the excretion of drugs can cause drugs to accumulate in the blood, so doses would need to be reduced.

Bioavailability is the amount of a drug and the rate at which that drug is available for circulation and so is able to produce a therapeutic effect. Bioavailability is typically measured using data from a blood concentration-time profile. When the blood concentration-time profile of a drug is compared to a blood concentration-time profile of an IV solution, it is called absolute bioavailability. If it is compared to anything other than an IV solution, it is called relative bioavailability.

Pharmacodynamics is the study of the biochemical and physiologic effects of drugs on the body. A **therapeutic window** is the range of doses that produces a therapeutic effect without causing significant adverse effects. The **duration of action** is how long a drug will be effective.

Generic and Brand Names

The brand name of a drug is the trademarked or advertised name of the drug. The generic name is essentially the chemical name of a drug. Generic drugs are imitations of brand name drugs; it must have the same active ingredients and formulation as the brand name drugs. Generic drugs' inactive ingredients may differ from brand name drugs. There is only one generic/non-proprietary name for a drug, but once its patent protection expires, it may be sold under multiple/different brand names.

See Appendix A: Top 200 Drugs for a list of the top generic and brand name drugs.

Therapeutic Equivalence

Pharmacy technicians should understand **therapeutic equivalence** to understand which drug can be substituted for another drug.

Two or more drugs are therapeutically equivalent if they meet the following criteria:
1. They have the same safety and efficacy.
2. They are pharmaceutically equivalent.
3. They are bioequivalent.
4. They are correctly labeled.
5. They manufactured in accordance with the FDA's Current Good Manufacturing Practice regulations.

Pharmaceutical equivalence is when two or more drugs contain the same amount of active ingredients. They must also have the same dosage form; route of administration; and meet similar standards of strength, purity, and quality. Pharmaceutical equivalents may differ in inactive ingredients, shape, scoring configuration, packaging, labeling, and date of expiration.

Bioequivalence is when two or more drugs have the same rates of absorption under similar conditions and dosages; essentially, they must have similar bioavailability.

The "Approved Drug Product with Therapeutic Equivalence Evaluations", also referred to as the "Orange Book", contains an official listing of therapeutically equivalent drugs.

Therapeutic Duplication

Therapeutic duplication is when multiple medications from the same class of drugs are prescribed for the same indication without clear directions for when one drug should be used over another. If multiple drugs from the same class are prescribed, each drug must have a specific indication or include criteria for the order in which the drugs should be taken.

Human Variability

Factors such as age, weight, gender, and genetics affects a person's response to medication.

- Up until the age of 12, children metabolize drugs faster; after the age of 12, their metabolism starts to slow down to normal adult levels.
- The elderly take more drugs which increases the likelihood of drug interactions. The elderly also experience more changes such as changes in gastric emptying time, impaired kidney function, etc.; all of which can affect how they respond to drugs.
- Due to hormonal differences and body composition (males have more muscles), males and females may respond differently to drugs.
- Pregnant women may experience delayed gastric emptying and decreased intestinal movement. The rate of urinary excretion is also increased.

Drug Interactions

Drug interactions occur when the effects of a drug are changed by another substance or drug when administered together. The following describes the different types of drug interactions.

Drug-Disease Interactions

Drug-disease interactions occur when a drug interacts or interferes with an existing medical condition. For example, beta-blockers taken for heart disease can worsen asthma; pseudoephedrine can increase the blood pressure of those with hypertension.

Drug-Drug Interactions

Drug-drug interactions occur when the effects of a drug are changed when taken with another drug. The interaction can be additive, synergistic, potentiated, or antagonistic. **Additive interaction** means the effect of two drugs is equal to the sum of the effect of the two drugs taken separately. **Synergistic interaction** means the effect of two drugs taken together is greater than the sum of the two drugs taken separately. **Potentiated interaction** occurs when one drug intensifies the actions of another drug. Two drugs are **antagonistic** when their interaction causes a decrease in the effects of one or both of the drugs. Both synergy and antagonism can occur during different phases of the interaction of multiple drugs.

Drug-Dietary Supplement Interactions

Dietary supplements can interfere with the way a drug acts or how the body absorbs, uses, or disposes of the drug. For example, ginseng can increase the bleeding effects of heparin, aspirin, and nonsteroidal anti-inflammatory drugs such as ibuprofen and naproxen.

Drug-OTC Interactions

Over-the-counter (OTC) drugs can interact with prescription drugs. For example, antihistamines, such as Benadryl, can cause drowsiness and intensify the sedative effects of prescription drugs such as diazepam, lorazepam, etc.

Drug-Food Interactions

Drug-food interactions occur when the effects of a drug are changed when taken with a particular food. An example of this is statins and grapefruit juice. Grapefruit juice should be avoided when taking statins because grapefruit juice decreases the metabolism of statins, causing a buildup of statins in the body which can lead to muscle and/or liver damage.

Drug-Nutrient Interactions

Drugs can interact with how the body absorbs, uses, and excretes nutrients. For example, Diuretics can cause potassium levels to be too low in your body.

Polypharmacy

Polypharmacy is the concurrent usage of multiple drugs. It is most common in the elderly, who are often being treated for multiple medical conditions.

Dosing

Dosage Forms and Physical Appearance

Dosage form describes the physical characteristics of a drug (e.g. tablet, capsule, solution, etc.). Below is a table of common dosage forms.

Form	Definition
capsules	Contains powder or liquid in a gelatin coating
elixirs	Active ingredients are mixed with a liquid, usually a kind of syrup or alcohol, in which they can dissolve. Does NOT need to be shaken before use.
emulsions	A mixture of 2 liquids that are immiscible (cannot be mixed without the help of external forces such mixing, stirring, shaking, or addition of an emulsifier)
ointment	An oily semi-solid prepared for topical use
suppositories	Solids that are inserted into the rectum, vagina, or urethra and dissolve. Can be used to provide local or systemic effects..
suspension	Active ingredients are mixed with a liquid, usually water, in which it cannot dissolve. Must be shaken before use.
tablets	Made from compressed powder of active and inactive ingredients
transdermal patch	A medicated adhesive patch placed on the skin to deliver medication through the skin and into the bloodstream

Routes of Administration

Oral

The oral route is the most often used route because it's the most convenient and usually safest and least expensive route. Drug absorption may begin in the mouth or stomach, but most drugs are absorbed through the small intestine. The disadvantage of taking drugs orally is that it may take longer to be absorbed and depending on what is in the digestive tract, the amount of medicine absorbed may vary.

Injection (Subcutaneous, Intramuscular, Intravenous, Intrathecal)

Drugs can be injected subcutaneously (under the skin), intramuscularly (in a muscle), intravenously (in a vein), or intrathecally (around the spinal cord).

To give a drug subcutaneously, a needle is inserted into fatty tissue just beneath the skin. The subcutaneous route is often used for drugs, such as protein drugs, that would be destroyed in the digestive tract if they were taken orally.

Drugs are given intramuscularly, instead of subcutaneously, when larger volumes of the drug are needed. It is typically injected into the muscle of the upper arm, thigh, or buttock. The larger the blood supply to the muscle, the faster the absorption.

Intravenous administration, a needle is inserted directly into a vein, is the best way to deliver a precise dose quickly and in a controlled manner throughout the body. It is also used for administering drugs which would cause pain and damage tissues if administered another way.

To administer a drug intrathecally, a needle is inserted between two vertebrae in the lower spine and into the space around the spinal cord. It is used when a drug is needed to produce rapid or local effects on the brain, spinal cord, or meninges.

Sublingual and Buccal

Drugs can be administered sublingually (placed under the tongue) or buccally (placed between the gums and cheek). Since the drugs are dissolved in the mouth and do not have to pass the intestinal wall, drug absorption into the bloodstream occurs rapidly.

Rectal

Drugs administered rectally, inserted into the rectum, are usually in suppository form. Because the rectum's wall is thin and its blood supply rich, the drug is rapidly absorbed. A suppository is often prescribed for people who cannot take a drug orally because they have nausea, cannot swallow, or as required before and after a surgery.

Vaginal

During vaginal administration, drugs are inserted into the vagina and slowly absorbed through the vaginal wall. It is often used to deliver estrogen to women during menopause.

Ocular

For ocular administration, drugs in the form of liquid, gel, or ointment are applied to the eyes. Ocular drugs are typically used for local, not systemic, effects. Liquid eye drops may run off too quickly for the drug to be absorbed well, but gels and ointments which keep the drug in contact with the eyes longer may blur vision.

Otic or Auricular

Ear drops are typically applied to the outer ear canal. Effects are local.

Nasal

During nasal administration, the drug is atomized (transformed into tiny droplets) and breathed in through the nose where it is absorbed by the lining of the nasal passage. Drugs administered this way are absorbed quickly, but may irritate the nasal passage.

Inhalation

Drugs are atomized into smaller droplets than those used for nasal administration and inhaled through the mouth and into the lungs. The smaller the droplets, the more is absorbed by the lungs. Few drugs are given this way because it often requires special equipment and is difficult to monitor the amount of drug absorbed.

Nebulization

Using special nebulizer devices, drugs are atomized or aerosolized into even smaller droplets and inhaled through the mouth and into the lungs. It can cause coughing and wheezing when the drug reaches the lungs. Nebulizers can also spread the droplets into the environment and affect others in the room.

Cutaneous

Drugs administered cutaneously are applied to the skin. They are commonly used to treat superficial skin disorders.

Transdermal

Drugs are delivered through an adhesive patch applied to the skin. Effects are systemic. A patch allows drugs to be delivered slowly and continuously over hours or days to keep levels of the drug in the body relatively constant.

Adverse Effects, Allergies, and Therapeutic Contraindications

An adverse effect is an unintended or undesired side effect of a drug. Adverse effects may be localized or systemic, mild or severe, or occur the first time taking a drug or after taking the drug for a while. Pharmaceutical manufacturers are required to report any serious unlabelled/unexpected adverse reactions to the FDA's MedWatch Program.

Some examples of side effects are:
- Allergies
- Carcinogenicity: the ability to cause cancer
- Teratogenicity: the ability to harm fetal development
- Hepatotoxicity: the ability to harm the liver
- Nephrotoxicity: the ability to harm the renal system
- Hematological effects (blood clotting, bleeding, etc.)
- Gastrointestinal effects (ulcers, nausea, diarrhea, etc.)
- Central Nervous System effects (drug dependence, tolerance, resistance)

Allergies

Allergic reactions to medicine can occur within minutes to weeks of drug administration. They can range from mild rashes to anaphylactic shock. Anaphylactic shock, which can be fatal, includes symptoms such as severe respiratory and circulatory distress. Emergency treatment with epinephrine is required for treating anaphylactic shock.

Symptoms of allergic reactions include:
- Hives/Rashes
- Swelling of face, throat, tongue or other areas
- Respiratory distress
- Circulatory distress

Therapeutic Contraindications

A therapeutic contraindication is a certain condition in which a drug should not be administered, or two drugs should not be administered together, as it may cause harm to the patient. Some common therapeutic contraindications are:

Alcohol	Alcohol should not be consumed with medication. Alcohol can worsen effects of drowsiness, nausea, loss of coordination, etc. If taken with depressants like benzodiazepines, it may severely depress the respiratory system. Alcohol, if taken with high doses of acetaminophen, may damage the liver.
Age	Some medications should not be given to children. For example, tetracycline

	is contraindicated in children because it can retard their growth.
Pregnancy	Many drugs are contraindicated during pregnancy because they can harm fetal development. Examples include tetracycline, isotretinoin, ACE inhibitors, and many more.

Dosage and Indication of Legend, OTC Medications, and Dietary Supplements

Dosage and Indication of Legend

Legend drugs are drugs that require a prescription. These drugs may or may not be considered abusable, but consultation with a medical professional that has prescribing authority is necessary. They are required to have the following legend on their label: "Caution: Federal Law prohibits dispensing without a prescription." or "Rx Only".

The indication of legend is the reason for which a drug is prescribed. The dosage may differ depending on the indication or reason for why a drug is being prescribed. If a drug is prescribed for reasons other than its indicated legend, its use is considered "off-label".

Dietary Supplements

Dietary supplements are not regulated by the FDA. Guidelines that dietary supplements must meet are found in the Dietary Health and Supplement Act of 1994.

OTC Medications

OTC medications, regulated by the FDA, do not require a prescription; however, their sale may still be restricted. Examples of OTC medications that have restricted access include emergency contraceptives or pseudoephedrine.

Because OTC drugs do not require a prescription, it is important to cross-check ingredients for drugs that are often used in multiple medicines to prevent overdosing. For example, acetaminophen is often used in medicine for colds as well a painkillers. Antihistamines may also be included in sleeping pills.

Medical Terminology

There are thousands of drugs in the pharmaceutical world and pharmacy technicians should be able to identify the main uses of a drug. One way to help pharmacy technicians identify the main use of a drug is to understand medical terminology. Many pharmaceutical and medical words are composed of a root, a suffix, and a prefix. The root gives meaning to the word and the prefixes and suffixes add or modify the meaning of the root. For example:

Entire Word	Prefix	Root	Suffix	Meaning
diplopia	Dipl (double)	Opia (vision)		Diplopia means "double vision"
gastritis		Gastr (stomach)	Itis (inflammation)	Gastritis means "inflammation of the stomach"
hypoglycemia	Hypo (low)	Glyc (sugar)	Emia (blood)	Hypoglycemia means "low blood sugar"

Common Prefixes

Prefix	Meaning	Prefix	Meaning
a	without	ambi	both
an	without	ante	before
anti	against	auto	self
bi	two or both	brady	slow
circum	around	cirrh	yellow
con	with	contra	against
dia	completely	dipl	double
dis	Separate, apart	dys	Painful, difficult
ec	Away or out of	ecto	outside
en	in	endo	within

epi	above	eso	inward
eu	Good, normal	exo	outside
hemi	half	heter	different
hyper	Above or over	hypo	Below, under
im	Not, without	immun	Having immunity
infra	Below, under	inter	between
intra	within	iso	equal
leuk	white	lip	fat
macro	large	mal	poor
medi	middle	melan	black
meso	middle	meta	Beyond, after
micro	small	mid	middle
mono	one	multi	many
neo	new	pachy	Heavy, thick
pan	all	para	Near, abnormal
peri	around	poly	many
post	after	pre	before
pro	before	pseudo	false
retro	after	super	above
supra	above	Sym, syn	with
tachy	fast	trans	across
tri	three	uni	one
xero	dry		

Common Suffixes

Suffix	Meaning	Suffix	Meaning

ac, al, ar, ary	pertaining to	algia	pain
asthenia	weakness	cele	Hernia, bulging
cyesis	pregnancy	dynia	pain
ectasis	dilation	ectomy	Surgical removal
edema	swelling	emesis	vomiting
emia	Blood condition	esthenia	Lack of sensation
genic	Producing, forming	gram	record
iatry	treatment	icle	small
itis	inflammation	lepsy	seizure
lith	stone	lysis	Breaking down
malacia	softening	megaly	enlargement
oma	tumor	opia, opsia	vision
orexia	appetite	paresis	Partial paralysis
pathy	disease	pepsia	digestion
phagia	swallowing	phasia	speech
philic	attraction	plegia	Paralysis, stroke
pnea	breathing	rrhage	To burst
rrhea	discharge	sclerosis	hardness
spasm	Involuntary contraction	stasis	Control, stop
stomy	Artificial opening	trophy	Nourishment, growth
urea	urination		

Common Root Words

Root	Meaning
acous, audi	hearing

adip	fat
alges	pain
andr	male
aneur	widening
angi	vessel
aort	aorta
arthr	joint
cardi	heart
carp	wrist
cere	cerebrum
crani	skull
cutane	skin
dactyl	Finger, toe
derm	skin
encephal	brain
esthes	sensation
gastr	stomach
gynec	woman
hem, hemat	blood
hepat	liver
hyster	uterus
ichthy	Dry, scaly
kerat	hard
lapar	abdomen
lord	curve
Mamm, mast	breast

my	muscle
myel	Spinal cord
necr	death
nephr	kidney
neur	nerve
ocul, ophthalm, optic	eye
pector	chest
ped, pod	foot
phalang	Bones of the fingers and toes
phas	speech
pneum	Lung, air
psycho	mind
pulmon	lung
onych	nail
oste	bone
prurit, psor	itching
rhin	nose
scoli	crooked,bent
somat	body
sten	narrow
stern	Sternum, breastbone
tars	ankle
thromb	clot
ven	vein

Drug Classifications

Drugs of similar classes often treat the same type of diseases or disorders and share the same United States Adopted Name (USAN) stem word. Each stem has hyphens at one or both ends of its text to show that it is found at the beginning, end, or in the middle of a generic name.

Analgesics

Analgesics are used to reduce pain. NSAIDs, salicylates, and Acetaminophen are often used to treat mild to moderate pain. Opiates are often used to treat severe pain. Common side effects include upset stomach, dizziness, loss of appetite, weakness. Common drug interactions include alcohol, blood thinners, MAO inhibitors, antidepressants.

USAN Stem	Definition	Example
-adom	analgesic	tifluadom
-buzone	anti-inflammatory/analgesic	phenylbutazone
-eridine	analgesic	meperidine
-fentanyl	narcotic analgesic	fentanyl derivatives
-profen	anti-inflammatory/analgesic	ibuprofen

Examples of Analgesics:

Type	Generic Name	Brand Name
salicylates	Acetylsalicylic acid (aspirin)	Bayer
NSAID	ibuprofen	Motrin
NSAID	naproxen	Aleve
Non-aspirin, non-nsaid	acetaminophen	Tylenol
opiate	morphine	Morphabond
opiate	meperidine	Demerol

Anesthetics

Anesthetic agents block or cause an absence of pain or sensation. There are two major types of anesthetics: local and general. Local anesthetics block pain conduction from peripheral nerves to the central nervous system, so it only affects a restricted area. General anesthetics depresses the central nervous system and causes unconsciousness.

USAN Stem	Definition	Example
-caine	Local anesthetics	lidocaine, procaine
-flurane	General inhalation anesthetics	isoflurane, sevoflurane, desflurane

Examples of local anesthetics:

Type	Generic Name	Brand Name
Ester	procaine	Novocain
Amide	lidocaine	Xylocaine
Amide	bupivacaine	Marcaine

Common general anesthetics:

Type	Generic Name	Brand Name
General Inhalation Anesthetic	isoflurane	Forane
General IV Anesthetic	propofol	Diprivan

Anti-Infectives

Anti-infective agents treat diseases caused by microorganisms such as bacteria, viruses, fungi, parasitic worms, etc.
- Antibiotics/Antimicrobials treat bacteria
- Antivirals treat viruses
- Antifungals treat fungi
- Antimycobacterials treat tuberculosis, leprosy, etc.
- Antiprotozoals treat malaria, vaginitis, etc.
- Anthelmintics treat parasitic worms

Antibiotics/Antimicrobials

Antibiotics/antimicrobials treat bacterial infections. They can either be bacteriostatic (inhibit bacterial growth) or bactericidal (kills bacteria). Many antibiotics decrease the effectiveness of birth control, cause photosensitivity, and have serious interactions with warfarin. Tetracyclines should not be used in children under 8 and during pregnancy. Those who have a sulfa allergy can react to antibiotics containing sulfa such as sulfamethoxazole-trimethoprim (Septra, Bactrim) and erythromycin-sulfisoxazole.

USAN Stem	Definition	Example
-cillin	Penicillin antibiotics	amoxicillin, ampicillin, dicloxacillin
-cycline	antibiotic	tetracycline
-monam	Monobactam antibiotics	gloximonam; oximonam; tigemonam
-mycin	antibiotic	daptomycin, erythromycin
-oxacin	antibiotic	difloxacin; ciprofloxacin
sulfa-	antibiotic	sulfonamide derivatives

Examples of antibiotics:

Type	Generic Name	Brand Name
antibiotic	amoxicillin	Amoxil, Moxatag, Trimox
antibiotic	ampicillin	Omnipen
antibiotic	cefaclor	Ceclor
antibiotic	cefixime	Suprax
antibiotic	erythromycin	Erythrocin
antibiotic	mupirocin	Bactroban
antibiotic	tetracycline	Tetracap

Antivirals

Antivirals treat viruses by inhibiting the replication of viruses. Common side effects include headache, nausea, muscle pain, vision problems. Common drug interactions include steroids and antihyperlipidemics.

USAN Stem	Definition	Example

-mantadine	antivirals	rimantadine; dopamantine
-motine	antivirals (quinoline derivatives)	famotine
vir-, -vir-, -vir	Antiviral substances (undefined group)	ganciclovir; enviradine; viroxime; alvircept; delavirdine
aril-, -aril, -aril-	Antiviral (arildone derivatives)	pleconaril; arildone; fosarilate
-uridine	antivirals	idoxuridine

Examples of antivirals:

Type	Generic Name	Brand Name
antiviral	acyclovir	Zovirax
antiviral	amantadine	Symmetrel
antiviral	oseltamivir	Tamiflu
antiviral	valacyclovir	Valtrex
antiviral/protease inhibitor	nelfinavir	Viracept

Antifungals

Antifungals kill fungi by preventing fungi cell permeability and access to nutrition. Long term usage of antifungals can lead to liver toxicity; monitoring liver function is required.

USAN Stem	Definition	Example
-conazole	Systemic antifungals (miconazole type)	fluconazole; oxiconazole
-fungin	Antifungal antibiotics (undefined group)	kalafungin

Examples of antifungals:

Type	Generic Name	Brand Name
antifungal	caspofungin	Cancidas

antifungal	fluconazole	Diflucan
antifungal	terbinafine	Lamisil
antifungal	itraconazole	Sporanox

Antineoplastics

Antineoplastic agents inhibit the growth of cancer cells. Side effects of antineoplastics include hair loss, immunosuppression, anema, GI ulcers, and weight loss. Major types of antineoplastic drugs include alkylating agents (nitrogen mustards), antimetabolites, plant alkaloids, hormones, antitumor antibiotics, and radioactive isotopes.

- Antimetabolites inhibit cell growth by interfering with a cells metabolic processes
- Alkylating agents bind with DNA and prevent cellular replication to inhibit growth
- Plant alkaloids may inhibit the enzyme topoisomerase which is required for cell growth
- Hormone therapy can be used to treat cancers that require certain hormones to grow
- Antitumor antibiotics interfere with the DNA inside cells to kill cancer cells
- Radioactive isotopes attach to cancer cells and release radiation that damages the cancer cells

USAN Stem	Definition	Example
-antrone	Antineoplastics; anthraquinone derivatives	pixantrone
-arabine	Antineoplastics (arabinofuranosyl derivatives)	fazarabine; fludarabine
-bulin	Antineoplastics (mitotic inhibitors; tubulin binders)	mivobulin
-fulven	Antineoplastic, acylfulven derivatives	viridofulven
-mustine	Antineoplastics (chloroethylamine derivatives)	carmustine
-rubicin	Antineoplastic antibiotics (daunorubicin type)	esorubicin; idarubicin

Examples of antineoplastics:

Type	Generic Name	Brand Name

antimetabolite	methotrexate	Rheumatrex
Alkylating agent/nitrosourea	carmustine	BiCNU
Hormone	tamoxifen	Nolvadex
Antitumor antibiotic	daunorubicin	Cerubidine

Cardiovascular Agents

Cardiovascular agents are used to treat diseases or disorders of the cardiovascular system. They can be classified by their mechanisms of action or the conditions they treat. The classifications by mechanism of actions are: beta-blockers, calcium channel blockers, diuretics, ACE inhibitors, and vasodilators.

- Beta blockers work by blocking the effects of the hormone epinephrine; it makes the heart beat with less force, reducing blood pressure. Beta blockers are used to treat high blood pressure and arrhythmias. Common side effects of beta blockers include: fatigue, cold hands, upset stomach, constipation, diarrhea, dizziness, shortness of breath, erectile dysfunction, bradycardia, hypotension, syncope. Common drug interactions include: amiodarone, clonidine, diltiazem, cyclosporine, digoxin, fluconazole, reserpine, MAO inhibitors, alcohol.
- Calcium channel blockers prevent calcium from entering cells of the heart and blood vessel walls, resulting in lower blood pressure. They are used to treat high blood pressure and arrhythmias. Common side effects include: dizziness, ankle/feet swelling, blurred vision, cough, fatigue, weight gain, cold sweats. Common drug interactions include: clarithromycin, cyclosporine, diltiazem, ritonavir, sildenafil, simvastatin, alcohol.
- Diuretics decrease blood volume (and thus blood pressure) by increasing the elimination of salts through increase urination. Diuretics can cause low levels of potassium. Common side effects include: dry mouth, muscle twitching, weakness, loss of appetite, tinnitus, upset stomach. Common drug interactions include: hormones, laxatives, antihypertensives, NSAIDs, ACE inhibitors, lithium, digoxin, diabetes drugs, methotrexate, chlorpropamide.
- ACE inhibitors reduce blood pressure by preventing your body from producing angiotensin II (a substance that narrows your blood vessels and raises your blood pressure). ACE inhibitors may cause coughing and high levels of potassium; there are special warnings for usage during pregnancy. Common side effects include: dry cough, nausea, loss of appetite, upset stomach. Common drug interactions include: other blood pressure medications, insulin, diabetes medication, NSAIDS, arthritis medication, alcohol.
- Vasodilators reduce blood pressure by relaxing and expanding blood vessels. Common side effects include: flushing, tachycardia/bradycardia, hypotension, heart palpitations, nausea, dizziness, increased hunger/thirst. Common drug interactions include: erectile dysfunction drugs, local anesthetics, tizanidine, phenytoin, blood thinner drugs, diuretics.

The classifications by the conditions they treat include antianginals, antiarrhythmics, antihypertensives, vasopressors, antihyperlipidemics, thrombolytics, and anticoagulants.

- Antianginals are used to treat angina (chest pain caused by narrowing of coronary arteries). Nitrates, beta-blockers, and calcium channel blockers are all antianginals.
- Antiarrhythmics are used to treat irregular heart rhythms. Beta-blockers and calcium channel blockers can also be used as an antiarrhythmic.
- Antihyperlipidemics are used to lower cholesterol levels.
- Antihypertensives are used to reduce blood pressure. Beta-blockers, diuretics, ACE inhibitors, and calcium channel blockers can be used to reduce blood pressure.
- Thrombolytics dissolve blood clots and anticoagulants prevent blood clots. Common anticoagulants include warfarin and heparin. Warfarin has many serious drug interactions (especially with aspirin) and overdosing can cause life threatening conditions. Too much vitamin K in your diet can lower the effect of warfarin. Avoid eating large amounts of leafy green vegetables, as many of them contain large amounts of vitamin K.
- Vasopressor are used to increase blood pressure; especially when the patient is in shock. Vasopressors may also be used to help supply blood to the brains and kidneys.

Many cardiovascular drugs interact with grapefruit juice.

USAN Stem	Definition	Example
-alol	Combined alpha and beta blockers	labetalol; medroxalol
-olol	Beta-blockers	timolol; atenolol
-fradil	Calcium channel blockers acting as vasodilators	mibefradil
-tiazem	Calcium channel blockers	diltiazem; clentiazem; iprotiazem
-pril	Antihypertensives (ACE inhibitors)	enalapril; temocapril; spirapril
-prilat	Antihypertensives (ACE inhibitors)	enalaprilat; spiraprilat
-crinat	Diuretics	brocrinat
-etanide	Diuretics	bumetanide
-pamide	Diuretics	alipamide
-semide	Diuretics	azosemide

-thiazide	Diuretics	chlorothiazide
dil-, -dil-, -dil	Vasodilators	fostedil
-dipine	Phenylpyridine vasodilators	darodipine; felodipine
-pamil	Coronary vasodilators	tiapamil
-sidomine	Antianginals	pirsidomine; molsidomine; linsidomine
-afenone	Antiarrhythmics	alprafenone; diprafenone
-aj-	Antiarrhythmics	lorajmine
-arone	Antiarrhythmics	amiodarone; dronedarone
-ilide	Class III antiarrhythmic agents	ibutilide; risotilide; dofetilide
-isomide	Antiarrhythmics	bidisomide
-fibrate	Antihyperlipidemics	bezafibrate
-imibe-	Antihyperlipidemics	eldacimibe; avasimibe; pactimibe
-vastatin	Antihyperlipidemics	atorvastatin; lovastatin; pravastatin
-azosin	Antihypertensives	doxazosin
-dralazine	Antihypertensives	hydralazine; endralazine
-arol	Anticoagulants	dicumarol
-irudin	Anticoagulants	desirudin
-xaban	Anticoagulants	tamixaban
-pressin	Vasoconstrictors (vasopressin derivatives)	desmopressin

Examples of cardiovascular agents:

Type	Generic Name	Brand Name
Beta-blocker	atenolol	Tenormin

Beta-blocker	metoprolol	Lopressor
Beta-blocker	nadolol	Corgard
Calcium channel blocker	amlodipine	Norvasc
Calcium channel blocker	diltiazem	Cardizem
Calcium channel blocker/ Antianginal	nifedipine	Procardia
Calcium channel blocker/ Vasodilator	verapamil	Isoptin
Diuretics	furosemide	Lasix
Diuretics	hydrochlorothiazide	Microzide
Diuretics	spironolactone	Aldactone
ACE inhibitor	benazepril	Lotensin
ACE inhibitor	captopril	Capoten
ACE inhibitor	enalapril	Vasotec
ACE inhibitor	lisinopril	Prinivil
Vasodilator	hydralazine	Apresoline
Antianginal	nitroglycerin	Nitrostat
Antiarrhythmic	amiodarone	Cordarone
Antiarrhythmic	digoxin	Lanoxin
Antihyperlipidemic	ezetimibe	Vytorin
Antihyperlipidemic	pravastatin	Pravachol
Antihyperlipidemic	simvastatin	Zocor
Antihypertensive	doxazosin	Cardura
Antihypertensive	hydralazine	Apresoline
Antihypertensive	prazosin	Minipress
Anticoagulant	heparin	Hep-Lock
Anticoagulant	warfarin	Coumadin

Anticoagulant	rivaroxaban	Xarelto

Endocrine Agents

Endocrine agents mimic naturally occurring hormones in the body like estrogens/androgens, thyroid hormones, corticosteroids, insulin, etc. They are usually prescribed to regulate hormonal imbalances.

- Hypoglycemics/Antihyperglycemics decrease blood glucose levels and help treat diabetes.
- Insulin, secreted by the pancreas, regulates blood glucose levels. Common side effects include headache, hunger, dizziness, shakiness, pale skin. Common drug interactions include alcohol.
- Glucagon, secreted by the pancreas, converts amino acids to glucose.
- Thyroid hormones such as levothyroxine and liothyronine sodium are used to treat hypothyroidism (a condition where the thyroid gland does not produce enough thyroid hormones).
- Antithyroid hormones such as methimazole and propylthiouracil are used to block thyroid hormone production to treat hyperthyroidism (a condition where the thyroid gland produces too much thyroid hormone).
- Corticosteroids, secreted by adrenal glands, are used to treat and control inflammation.

USAN Stem	Definition	Example
-formin	Hypoglycemics	metformin
-gliptin,-glitazone	Antihyperglycemics	vildagliptin, ciglitazone

Examples of endocrine agents:

Type	Generic Name	Brand Name
hypoglycemic	metformin	Glucophage
antihyperglycemic	rosiglitazone	Avandia
Thyroid hormone	levothyroxine	Synthroid
Antithyroid hormone	methimazole	Tapazole
Corticosteroids	hydrocortisone	Cortef
Corticosteroids	prednisone	Sterapred
Insulin	glargine	Lantus

Dermatological Agents

Dermatological agents are used to treat skin disorders and diseases.

USAN Stem	Definition	Example
-cort	Steroid (Cortisone derivative)	hydrocortisone
-olone, -onide	Steroids	triamcinolone, fluocinonide
-conazole	Antifungal	miconazole

Examples of dermatological agents:

Type	Generic Name	Brand Name
Steroid (Cortisone derivative)	hydrocortisone	Cortef
Steroid	fluocinonide	Lidex
Antifungal	ciclopirox	Penlac
Antifungal	miconazole	Monistat
Antibiotic	mupirocin	Bactroban
Antibiotic	bacitracin	Baciguent
Acne Treatment	clindamycin	Cleocin
Acne Treatment	tretinoin	Retin-A
Antihistamine	diphenhydramine	Benadryl
Cold Sore Treatment	acyclovir	Zovirax
Cold Sore Treatment	docosanol	Abreva

Gastrointestinal Agents

Gastrointestinal agents treat issues with the stomach and/or intestines; classes of gastrointestinal agents includes enzymes, antidiarrheals, antiemetics (anti-vomiting), antiulcer, laxatives, and stool softeners.

- Enzymes can be prescribed to help with digestion and nutrition absorption.
- Antidiarrheals help treat diarrhea.

- Antiemetics treat nausea and vomiting.
- Antacids are used to neutralize stomach acids to help with indigestion symptoms.
- Antiulcer agents are used to reduce the production of stomach acids.
- Laxatives and stool softeners are used to treat constipation. Laxatives can be bulk forming, stimulant (irritate the intestinal lining and nerves), saline (increase intestinal water absorption for softer stools), osmotic (increase stool water content through osmosis).

USAN Stem	Definition	Example
-prazole, -glumide	antiulcer	Lansoprazole, amiglumide
-aldrate	antacid	magaldrate
-ase	enzymes	alglucerase; dornase

Examples of gastrointestinal agents:

Type	Generic Name	Brand Name
antacid	magaldrate	Riopan, Lowsium
antacid	calcium carbonate	Tums, Rolaids
antiulcer	lansoprazole	Prevacid
antiulcer	omeprazole	Prilosec
enzyme	pancrelipase	Creon
enzyme	alglucerase	Ceredase
antiemetic	ondansetron	Zofran
antiemetic	promethazine	Phenergan
antidiarrheal	loperamide	Imodium
antidiarrheal	diphenoxylate, atropine	Lomotil
antidiarrheal	bismuth subsalicylate	Pepto Bismol
stool softener	docusate	Colace
laxative	bisacodyl	Dulcolax
laxative	psyllium	Metamucil

Hematological Agents

Hematopoietics are used to stimulate blood cell growth and treat anemia. Hemostatic drugs are used to prevent excessive bleeding.

Examples of hematological agents:

Type	Generic Name	Brand Name
Hematopoietic	ferumoxytol	Feraheme
Hematopoietic	ferrous sulfate	Slow Fe
Hemostatic	aminocaproic acid	Amicar
Hemostatic	tranexamic acid	Lysteda

Musculoskeletal Agents

Musculoskeletal agents treat a wide variety of conditions including pain, rheumatoid arthritis, osteoporosis, gout, etc.

- Rheumatoid arthritis is typically first treated with NSAIDs which reduces inflammation and pain. As the condition worsens, the disease may be treated with antirheumatic drugs such as methotrexate. Antirheumatic drugs may cause nausea, cramping, and diarrhea.
- Muscle relaxant/antispasmodic side effects often include dizziness, drowsiness, and weakness. Common drug interactions include alcohol, sedatives, MAO inhibitors, opiates.
- Gout, which may cause joint swelling and pain, is treated with uricosuric drugs which increase uric acid elimination and xanthine oxidase inhibitors which interfere with uric acid synthesis. Common side effects include nausea and diarrhea. Common drug interactions include alcohol, blood thinners, antihyperlipidemics, antibiotics.
- Bisphosphonates are used in the treatment of osteoporosis; they increase bone density by reducing bone resorption. Common side effects include cough, sore throat, mild bone pain, stomach upset. Common drug interactions include NSAIDs, antibiotics, diuretics, steroids, cancer medications.

USAN Stem	Definition	Example
-dronate	bisphosphonates	ibandronate

Examples of musculoskeletal agents:

Type	Generic Name	Brand Name
antirheumatic	adalimumab	Humira
antirheumatic	leflunomide	Arava
antirheumatic	methotrexate	Rheumatrex
antigout/uricosuric	probenecid	Benemid
antigout/xanthine oxidase inhibitor	allopurinol	Zyloprim
osteoporosis	ibandronate	Boniva
osteoporosis	risedronate	Actonel
osteoporosis	alendronate	Fosamax
Muscle relaxant	cyclobenzaprine	Flexeril
Muscle relaxant	tizanidine	Zanaflex

Neurological Agents

Common neurological disorders you will encounter include: Parkinson's disease, Alzheimer's, epilepsy, multiple sclerosis, migraines, and attention deficit hyperactivity disorder (ADHD).

- Parkinson's disease is a progressive neuromuscular condition associated tremors, slowness of movements, and low levels of dopamine. Most Parkinson's medication is aimed at increasing dopamine levels through one of the following manners:
    - Dopamine agonists such as bromocriptine, pramipexole, and ropinirole bind to and activate dopamine receptors.
    - Drugs such as levodopa provide exogenous dopamine to the brain.
    - Carbidopa is a decarboxylase inhibitor. It prevents levodopa from being broken down before it reaches the brain.
    - Anticholinergics are used to treat tremors.
    - Common side effects of Parkinson's drugs include nausea, orthostatic hypotension, and dyskinesia (involuntary movements).
- Alzheimer's is a progressive disorder associated with loss of memory and cognition. Most Alzheimer's medications aim at slowing the breakdown of acetylcholine or slowing the buildup of glutamate. Antidepressants are also often prescribed to patients with Alzheimer's as they often also suffer from depression.
    - Donepezil, rivastigmine, and tacrine work by increasing acetylcholine activity.
    - Galantamine works by slowing the breakdown of acetylcholine.

- Common side effects of anti-Alzheimer's drugs include dizziness, confusion, fatigue, and headaches.
- Common drug interactions include NSAIDs, anti-arrhythmia drugs, bethanechol, phenytoin, metformin, quinidine, sodium bicarbonate.
- ADHD is associated with inability to focus and hyperactivity. Most ADHD drugs act as stimulants or non-stimulants.
  - Stimulants, such as lisdexamfetamine and dexmethylphenidate, increase dopamine levels and can cause restlessness, insomnia, mood swings, etc.
  - Non-stimulants, such as atomoxetine, increase norepinephrine.
  - Common side effects include dry mouth, nausea, weight loss, insomnia.
  - Common drug interactions include MAO inhibitors, blood thinners, antidepressants, diuretics, antiepileptics.
- Epilepsy is a neurological disorder associated with recurring seizures. It is typically treated with antiepileptic drugs (phenytoin, phenobarbital, albutoin) and anticonvulsant drugs (carabersat; tidembersat). Common side effects include: anxiety, blurred vision, nausea, dry mouth, drowsiness. Common drug interactions include: diuretics, metformin, lithium, blood thinners, other antiepileptics, rifampin, albendazole, digoxin, antidepressants, antihyperlipidemics.
- Multiple Sclerosis is a disorder in which the brain and spinal cord nerve cell covers are attacked by the immune system. Immunomodulators (interferon beta-1-a/b, ivarimod, ancriviroc) are used to prevent new attacks.
- Migraine headaches are often treated with anti-inflammatory drugs such as aspirin, NSAIDS, and a class of drugs called "triptans". Common side effects include muscle pain/weakness, dizziness, irritability, upset stomach. Common drug interactions include dopamine, antihypertensives, HIV/AIDS drugs, other triptan drugs.

USAN Stem	Definition	Example
-bersat	anticonvulsant	carabersat, tidembersat
-toin, -bamate	antiepileptic	albutoin,meprobamate, felbamate
-imod, -criviroc	immunomodulators	ivarimod; pidotimod; ancriviroc
-pezil	anti-alzheimer	icopezil; donepezil
-ditan, -triptan	antimigraine	alniditan;naratriptan; oxitriptan; sumatriptan

Examples of neurological agents:

Type	Generic Name	Brand Name
antiparkinsonian	Carbidopa, levodopa	Sinemet
antiparkinsonian	pramipexole	Mirapex
antiparkinsonian	ropinirole	Requip
anticholinergic	benztropine	Cogentin
anti-alzheimer	donepezil	Aricept
anti-alzheimer	memantine	Namenda
antiepileptic	phenytoin	Dilantin
antiepileptic	felbamate	Felbatol
immunomodulators	pidotimod	Pilimod
immunomodulators	interferon beta-1a	Avonex
immunomodulators	interferon beta-1a	Betaseron
ADHD	methylphenidate	Ritalin
ADHD	dextroamphetamine, amphetamine	Adderall
ADHD	atomoxetine	Strattera
antimigraine	ibuprofen	Motrin
antimigraine	rizatriptan	Maxalt
antimigraine	sumatriptan	Imitrex

Ophthalmic (Eye) Agents

Common eye conditions or disorders you may encounter include glaucoma (abnormally high eye pressure that can damage the optic nerve), conjunctivitis ("pink eye"), and dry eyes.

- Glaucoma is treated with drugs that reduce eye pressure such as brimonidine and betaxolol. Glaucoma drugs are typically used long term.
- Conjunctivitis is highly contagious. If the conjunctivitis is due to a bacterial infection, it may be treated with antibiotics such as gentamicin, ciprofloxacin, and sodium sulfacetamide. If it is due to an allergy, it may be treated with histamine blockers such as levocabastine and olopatadine.

- Inflammation of the eye may be treated with corticosteroids (budesonide, prednisolone, etc.) and NSAIDs (flurbiprofen, ketorolac, etc.).
- Hydroxypropyl cellulose is used to treat dry eyes.

Drugs that treat eye conditions are typically in drop or ointment dosage form. When applying eye drops:
- Always wash your hands before applying eye drops.
- Never allow the applicator to touch the eye and never touch the applicator top.
- Do not rub the eyes.
- If you need to apply more than one type of eye drop or ointment, wait the suggested amount of time between applications; typically, 5 minutes between solutions and 10-15 minutes between ointments.

USAN Stem	Definition	Example
-olol	antiglaucoma	betaxolol, metipranolol, timolol
-astine	antihistamine	levocabastine, emedastine

Examples of ophthalmic agents:

Type	Generic Name	Brand Name
antiglaucoma	betaxolol	Betoptic
antiglaucoma	bimatoprost	Lumigan
antiglaucoma	latanoprost	Xalatan
antihistamine	levocabastine	Livostin
antihistamine	azelastine	Optivar
antihistamine	olopatadine	Patanol
antibiotics	ciprofloxacin	Ciloxan
antibiotics	gentamicin	Garamycin
anti-inflammation	prednisolone	Pred Forte
anti-inflammation	flurbiprofen	Ocufen
eye lubricant	N/A	Lacrisert

eye lubricant	propylene glycol	Systane

Otic (Ear) Agents

Otic agents are often used to treat ear infections and ear wax accumulation; they are typically in drop or ointment dosage form.

Examples of otic agents:

Type	Generic Name	Brand Name
Ear wax softener/remover	carbamide peroxide	Debrox
Ear wax softener/remover and ear infection treatment	acetic acid	VoSol
Ear infection	neomycin, polymyxin b, hydrocortisone	Cortisporin Otic
Ear infection	Ciprofloxacin, dexamethasone	Ciprodex

Psychotropic Agents

Psychotropic agents are drugs that affect the mind, emotion, and behavior. Some common psychological disorders include anxiety, depression, bipolar disorder, and schizophrenia.

- Bipolar disorder is characterized by extreme mood swings (mania and depression). It is treated with antipsychotic drugs such as quetiapine and risperidone and mood stabilizers such as lithium.
- Schizophrenia is a psychological disorder characterized by thoughts or experiences that are out of touch with reality. It is treated with antipsychotic drugs. Common side effects include: tremors, weight gain/loss, headache, nausea, appetite changes, restlessness. Common drug interactions include: alcohol, antihypertensives, anti-parkinson, benzodiazepines.
- Anxiety is characterized by extreme fear or worry. It is treated using anti-anxiety medication. Common side effects include: depression, confusion, dizziness, fatigue, habit forming. Common drug interactions include: alcohol, opiates, cold medications, antihistamines, contraceptives.
- Depression is a mental disorder characterized by persistent depressed mood and lost of interest in daily activities. It is treated using antidepressants. Common side effects include: headache, drowsiness, insomnia, decreased sex drive, dry mouth, weight gain or loss. Common drug interactions include: alcohol, MAO inhibitors, beta-blockers, warfarin, antidiabetics, antiepileptics.

- Sedatives are used to treat insomnia and relax/calm a person. Common side effects include: depression, confusion, dizziness, fatigue, habit forming. Common drug interactions include: alcohol, opiates, cold medications, antihistamines, contraceptives.

USAN Stem	Definition	Example
-azepam, -perone, -axine	anti-anxiety agents	lorazepam, duoperone, loratadine
-pidem, -plon	hypnotics/sedatives	zolpidem; alpidem; ocinaplon; zaleplon
-peridol, -peridone, -troline	antipsychotic	haloperidol; risperidone; iloperidone; ocaperidone; quetiapine; carvotroline; gevotroline
-oxetine, -pramine, -triptyline	antidepressants	dapoxetine; seproxetine; lofepramine; amitriptyline

Examples of psychotropic drugs:

Type	Generic Name	Brand Name
mood stabilizer	lithium	Lithobid
antipsychotic	haloperidol	Haldol
antipsychotic	risperidone	Risperdal
antipsychotic	clozapine	Clozaril
anti-anxiety	lorazepam	Ativan
anti-anxiety	diazepam	Valium
anti-anxiety	alprazolam	Xanax
antidepressant	duloxetine	Cymbalta
antidepressant	fluoxetine	Prozac
antidepressant	sertraline	Zoloft
sedative	eszopiclone	Lunesta
sedative	zaleplon	Sonata

sedative	zolpidem	Ambien

Reproductive Agents

Reproductive agents can be used to regulate sex hormone balances, increase fertility, prevent conception, etc.

Common side effects of estrogen hormone therapy include hot flashes, breast tenderness/changes, dizziness, acne, unusual hair growth, change in sexual desire. Common drug interactions include alcohol and other hormone medications.

USAN Stem	Definition	Example
extr-	estrogens	estradiol

Examples of reproductive agents:

Type	Generic Name	Brand Name
Hormone replacement	testosterone	Androgel
Hormone replacement	estradiol	Vagifem
Hormone replacement	medroxyprogesterone	Provera
Ovary Stimulant	clomiphene	Clomid
Contraceptive (norethindrone and ethinyl estradiol)	nortrel 7/7/7	Ortho Novum
Contraceptive (drospirenone and ethinyl estradiol)	gianvi	Yav
Contraceptive (norelgestromin and ethinyl estradiol)	xulane	Ortho Evra Patch

Respiratory Agents

Respiratory agents are used to treat conditions such as asthma, emphysema, bronchitis, colds, and allergies. They include antihistamines, decongestants, antitussives, expectorants, and bronchodilators.

- Antihistamines are used to treat allergies by reducing inflammation, itching, etc. Antihistamines can cause drowsiness.
- Decongestants treat nose stuffiness by causing mucous membrane vasoconstriction.
- Expectorants thin mucus so that it's easier to cough up and relieve chest congestion.
- Bronchodilators ("inhalers") help treat asthma by dilating the bronchi to make it easier to breathe. Common side effects include dry mouth and throat, shakiness, restlessness. Common drug interactions include diuretics, MAO inhibitors, antihypertensives.
- Antitussives are used to treat productive and non-productive coughs; it is available in narcotic and non-narcotic preparations. Narcotic antitussives can cause severe drowsiness.

USAN Stem	Definition	Example
-ast	antiasthmatics/antiallergics (not acting as antihistamines)	cinalukast; pobilukast; montelukast
-atadine, -tibant	antiasthmatics	olopatadine; loratadine; icatibant
-astine, -azoline	antihistamine	ebastine; antazoline
-terol	bronchodilators	albuterol

Examples of respiratory agents:

Type	Generic Name	Brand Name
antiasthmatic	montelukast	Singulair
bronchodilator	albuterol	Ventolin
bronchodilator	theophylline	Theo-24
antihistamine	loratadine	Claritin
antihistamine	promethazine	Phenergan
antitussive	dextromethorphan	Delsym
antitussive	hydrocodone, chlorpheniramine	Tussionex
decongestant	pseudoephedrine	Sudafed
decongestant	phenylephrine	Sudafed-PE
expectorant	guaifenesin	Robitussin, Mucinex

Urinary Tract Agents

Urinary tract agents treat conditions like urinary incontinence, difficulty urinating, painful urination, etc.

- Antimuscarinic agents are used to treat urinary incontinence or overactive bladders by preventing or reducing bladder contractions.
- Phosphodiesterase (PDE) inhibitors treat male impotence by increasing blood flow to the penis after sexual stimulation. Common side effects include prolonged erection, headache, nausea. Common drug interactions include nitrates.
- Alpha blockers relax the muscles of the prostate and bladder to help with difficulty urinating. Common side effects include headache and trouble getting/maintaining an erection. Common drug interactions include antihypertensives, antivirals, antifungals.

USAN Stem	Definition	Example
-afil	PDE inhibitors	sildenafil

Examples of urinary tract agents:

Type	Generic Name	Brand Name
PDE inhibitors	sildenafil	Viagra
PDE inhibitors	tadalafil	Cialis
Alpha blocker	tamsulosin	Flomax
Alpha blocker	finasteride	Proscar
Overactive bladder treatment	solifenacin	Vesicare
Overactive bladder treatment	tolterodine	Detrol

Vaccines

Common side effects of vaccines include soreness, redness/swelling/pain at injection site, low grade fever.

Examples of vaccines:

Vaccine	Brand Name

Diphtheria, Tetanus, Pertussis (DTaP)	Daptacel, Tripedia
Haemophilus influenzae type B (Hib)	Liquid Pedvax HIB, ActHIB
Hepatitis A	Havrix, VAQTA
Hepatitis B	Engerix-B, Recombivax HB
Influenza	FluMist, Afluria, Fluarix
Measles, Mumps, Rubella (MMR)	Attenuvax, MMR II, Mumpsvax
Varicella	Varivax
Hib and Hep B combo	Comvax
DTaP and Hep B and IPV combo	Pediarix
MMR and Varicella combo	ProQuad
DTaP and Hib combo	TriHIBit

Pharmacy Law and Regulations

There are two main agencies involved in the regulation of pharmacies: The Food and Drug Administration (FDA) and the Drug Enforcement Administration (DEA). The FDA's responsibility is to assure the safety, efficacy, and quality of drugs, medical devices, food, cosmetics, dietary supplements, and products that give off radiation. The DEA's responsibility is the enforcement of the Controlled Substances Act.

Local, State, and Federal Law Reconciliation

Pharmacies must follow all local, state, and federal laws. If the laws disagree, the most strict law must be followed. If a pharmacy technician fails to observe a law, the supervising pharmacist is subject to a penalty by the state board.

Controlled Substances

The Controlled Substances Act requires manufacturers, distributors, or dispensers of controlled substances to register with the DEA. There are 5 classes of controlled substances: Schedules I, II, III, IV, and V. Some states require Schedule II drugs to be stored in a locked narcotics cabinet. Schedule III, IV, and V drugs may be kept openly on storage shelves. Prescriptions and stock bottles containing controlled substances may have a red "C" stamp to indicate the presence of a controlled substance.

Controlled Substances Classes/Schedules

Controlled Substance Class	Definition
Schedule I	Drugs that have a high risk for abuse and have no medical use. They cannot be prescribed. Examples: heroin, hallucinogenic substances.
Schedule II	Drugs that have a high risk for abuse, but also have accepted medical use. Examples: Amphetamines, methadone, cocaine, morphine.
Schedule III	Drugs that have less risk than Schedule I and II substances, but have accepted medical use and may lead to low or moderate physical/psychological dependence. Example: anabolic steroids, ketamine.

Schedule IV	Drugs that have a less risk than Schedule III drugs, but have accepted medical use and may lead to limited physical/psychological dependence. Examples: chloral hydrate, propoxyphene, clonazepam.
Schedule V	Drugs that have less risk than Schedule IV drugs,but have accepted medical use and may lead to limited physical/psychological dependence. Examples: drugs with no more than 200 mg of codeine per 100 mL or per 100g, diphenoxylate.

Controlled Substances Documentation Requirements (DEA)

Receiving, Ordering, and Returning Controlled Substances Requirements

Schedule III, IV, and V do not require special forms. They may be ordered online, over the phone, or via fax.

The DEA 222 form, a triplicate form, is used to receive, order, or return Schedule II controlled substances. It must be filled out in pen, typewriter, or indelible pencil and signed by the person registered with the DEA. If a mistake is made, do not alter the form; instead, start a new form. Copy 1 (the top copy) is retained by the supplier, Copy 2 is sent to the DEA, and Copy 3 is retained by the purchaser (the pharmacy). Copy 3 must contain the number of containers received and the date it was received. All forms, even those that are incomplete or illegible, must be kept for 2 years.

Destruction of Controlled Substances Requirements

To destroy controlled substances, you must use a DEA 41 form. On the form, you must provide the following information:
- DEA registration number, name, address, phone number
- NDC number, names, strengths, forms, and quantities of controlled substances that will be destroyed
- Date, location, and method of destruction
- Signatures of 2 witnesses who are authorized employees

Loss/Theft of Controlled Substances Requirements

If a controlled substance is lost or stolen, the pharmacy must notify the nearest DEA diversion office and the local police department. It must also fill out a DEA 106 form; the original form is sent to the DEA and a copy is kept by the pharmacy.

Prescription Restrictions

Schedule II, III, IV, and V prescriptions must contain the prescriber's signature in ink or a digital signature.

Schedule II

Schedule II prescriptions must be presented in person at the pharmacy and prescriptions must be signed manually in ink. The only exception is if the patient:
- Lives in a long term care facility or community based care
- Is in hospice care
- Receives compounded home infusion or IV pain therapy.

In such cases, the prescription may be faxed; the prescriber's signature must be on the fax.

Schedule II prescriptions are valid for 7 days, after which, the prescriber must write a new prescription. Prescriptions can only be written for, at most, a 30 day supply and no refills.

The following Schedule II prescription changes can be made, by a prescriber to a pharmacist, over the phone: dosage form, strength, amount of medical prescribed, directions for taking medication.

The following changes can NOT be made to Schedule II prescriptions, even if requested by a physician: patient's name (spelling, etc.), change in controlled substance prescribed.

Schedule III, IV, or V

Schedule III, IV, or V prescriptions may be sent electronically and in some states, they may be faxed or phoned into the pharmacy.

Refill Restrictions

Schedule II prescriptions may not be refilled. Partial or emergency fills for Schedule II drugs may be dispensed if the pharmacist does not have enough supply to dispense the full amount; the remaining amount must be dispensed within 72 hours. Emergency fills may not exceed a 3 day supply. For partial fills, the pharmacist must write down the quantity dispensed on the front of the prescription and a new prescription must be presented to receive the remaining quantity. The prescriber must be notified if the prescription is not picked up within 72 hours.

Schedule III or IV prescriptions may be refilled up to 5 times within 6 months after the issue date. Schedule III or IV prescriptions can be partially filled any amount of time so long as the total quantity dispensed matches the total quantity prescribed within the 6 months.

Schedule V and non-controlled drugs may be refilled as specified by the prescriber.

Transfer Restrictions

All original and transferred prescriptions must be kept for 2 years. All transferred prescriptions must be communicated between pharmacists.

Schedule II prescriptions cannot be transferred. If the pharmacies do NOT share an online database, Schedule III, IV, and V original prescriptions may be transferred one time between the pharmacies. If the pharmacies share an online database, then Schedule III, IV, and V prescriptions may be transferred the same number of times as the maximum number of refills on the original prescription.

To transfer a prescription, a pharmacist must write "void" on the front of the prescription; on the back, the pharmacist must write the name, address, receiving pharmacist's name, and DEA number of the receiving pharmacy.

The receiving pharmacist should write "transfer" on the front of the prescription and record the original prescription issuance date; number of refills; original dispensing date; number of refills remaining; transferring pharmacy's name, address, and DEA number; name of pharmacist who received the transferred prescription.

Record Keeping, Documentation, and Retention

The Board of Pharmacy has the authority to inspect logs or records at any time.

Schedule II prescription records must be kept separate from the records of all other prescription types. All paper prescription records must be kept for 2 years. All electronic logs/inventory must be kept permanently.

All invoices for controlled substances must be signed, dated, stamped with a red "C", and kept for 2 years.

An inventory record must be kept and maintained for 2 years. Inventory of Schedule II drugs must be kept in a separate file from inventory of Schedule III, IV, and V drugs. Schedule II drugs must be counted exactly, but Schedule III, IV, and V drugs can be estimated. The exception to the estimated count would be for containers that hold more than 1,000 tablets or capsules. In that case, an exact count of the contents of the container must be undertaken.

Restricted Drug Programs and Prescription-Processing Requirements

Isotretinoin Safety and Risk Management Act

Isotretinoin (Accutane) can cause serious adverse effects such as fetal abnormalities and death. Everyone who prescribes, dispenses, or uses isotretinoin (Accutane) must register with iPledge. Reportings of adverse side effects must be reported on a quarterly basis and also within 15 days of the incident. All centers are evaluated annually for program compliance.

Before a patient receives their prescription, they must do the following:
1. Register with iPledge
2. Receive counseling from Pharmacist about the risks of taking the drugs and requirements for use.
3. Sign a consent form.
4. Comply with all pregnancy testing and choose 2 types of birth control.
5. Get a blood test before and 30 days after treatment.

Isotretinoin prescriptions:
1. Must be presented in person.
2. Must be written in 30 day durations.
3. Must be filled and picked up with 7 days (date of the pregnancy test is considered the first day).

To get isotretinoin refills, female patients need to take monthly pregnancy tests, specify methods of birth control, and answer questions about the iPledge program.

Thalidomide

The System For Thalidomide Education and Prescribing Safety (STEPS) is used when prescribing Thalidomide. Before receiving their first prescription, a patient must register for STEPS, take a pregnancy test, and received mandatory counseling. To get refills, a patient must continue taking regular pregnancy tests and receiving counseling.

Clozapine

Patients who take clozapine must have their white blood cell counts regularly monitored. Both the pharmacist and prescriber must have access to the results of the white blood cell count.

Formula to Verify the Validity of a DEA number

DEA numbers are required on all controlled substance prescriptions; they should not be used on non-controlled prescriptions.

DEA numbers consist of 2 letters and 7 numbers. The first letter represents the type of registrant (e.g., M for mid-level practitioner). The second letter is the first letter of the prescriber's last name. To verify that the DEA number is valid, perform the following steps:
1. Add the 1st, 3rd, and 5th numbers; we'll call this SumOfGroup1.
2. Add the 2nd, 4th, and 6th numbers; we'll call this SumOfGroup2.
3. Multiply SumOfGroup2 by 2; we'll call this Group2Doubled.
4. Add SumOfGroup1 and Group2Doubled; we'll call this the FinalValue.
5. The last digit in the FinalValue is called the "check digit" number and it should match the last digit in the DEA number.

Example:
DEA Number: AB2453671
1. 2 + 5 + 6 = 13
2. 4 + 3 + 7 = 14
3. 14 * 2 = 28
4. 13 + 28 = 41
5. This is valid because the last digit of 41 is 1, which matches the last digit of the DEA number.

Behind the Counter OTC Medications

The Combat Methamphetamine Epidemic Act (CMEA) requires all OTC drugs that contain ephedrine and pseudoephedrine to be kept behind the pharmacy counter. It also places a limit on the amount of ephedrine or pseudoephedrine that can be sold to an individual (3.6 grams per day and 9 grams per month, of which no more than 7.5 grams may be imported through a contract carrier or the US Postal Service). Purchasers must show a photo id when purchasing and pharmacies must keep information (product name, quantity sold, buyer name/address/id/signature, date/time of sale) about the buyer for at least 2 years after each purchase. MethCheck allows pharmacies to keep track of transactions involving ephedrine and/or pseudoephedrine.

Exempt narcotics are drugs that contain habit forming ingredients, but are allowed to be sold without a prescription to those who are 18 years or older. They MUST be dispensed by a pharmacist, but a pharmacy technician can perform the cash register transaction. Purchasers must provide identification and there is a limit to how much they can purchase in a 48 hour period. Pharmacies must maintain a record containing information (product name, quantity sold, buyer name/address/id/signature, date/time of sale, name or initial of pharmacist who dispensed the drug) about each purchase.

Emergency Contraceptives

Emergency contraceptives are not kept behind pharmacy counters, but there are restrictions on their sale. Plan B One-Step, an emergency contraceptive, has dual marketing status. Dual marketing status means a drug has both prescription and OTC drug status.

Requirement for Consultation (OBRA)

The Omnibus Budget Reconciliation Act (OBRA) requires that pharmacist provide patient counseling. Federal laws require that all Medicaid patients be counseled, but most state laws require that non-Medicaid patients be counseled as well. OBRA requires that all states have a Prospective Drug Review (DUR) program where pharmacist must document information (common side effects, drug contraindications and interactions, dosage and duration of therapy, etc.) and present the information to a patient orally and in written form.

Data Integrity, Security, and Confidentiality

HIPAA

The Health Insurance Portability and Accountability Act (HIPAA) protects patient privacy and regulates the transfer of all patient health information electronically, on paper, or orally. It regulates how and when pharmacies and other healthcare providers may use and disclose a patient's protected health information (PHI). PHI includes information such as name, address, date of birth, medical history, insurance number, etc. Information stored or transmitted must have safeguards in place to prevent illegal access to the information. Pharmacies must provide patients with written notice of their privacy procedures and the patients' privacy rights.

HIPAA requires all healthcare providers to have a National Provider Identifier (NPI), a ten digit number, that stays with the provider for life. Healthcare providers must use their NPI in all transactions covered by HIPAA.

HIPAA does allow pharmacies to disclose PHI (the minimum necessary), WITHOUT patient approval, to others who are working on behalf of the patient such as physician offices and insurance/benefits management companies. All people who have access to PHI must be trained regarding HIPAA annually, even personnel that only come to service computers.

Data Integrity

For data integrity, it's important that all data is entered and recorded accurately. It is also important that any changed information is attribute to the correct person with the correct date and time.

Security

Information must be secured, not only in storage or on a computer, but also when information is transmitted electronically or otherwise.

Data Backup and Archiving

To prevent loss of data, the pharmacy computer servers should be backed up daily. In case of fires or natural disasters, the backups should be stored at a different location.

FDA's Recall Classifications

Vaccine Adverse Event Reporting System (VAERS) is a program maintained by the FDA to monitor vaccines. MedWatch is a program maintained by the FDA that allows healthcare professionals to report adverse effects of a drug. An adverse effect is a negative unintended side effect of a drug. If the FDA deems it necessary, it may seek an injunction to prevent the manufacturer from distributing the drug; it may seize the drug; or it may issue a recall of the drug. An injunction is a court order to prevent an action. A recall involves removing the drug from the market.

There are 3 recall classifications: Class I, Class II, Class III.
Class I: There is a strong likelihood that the product will cause serious adverse effects or death.
Class II: Product may cause temporarily but reversible adverse effects or there is little likelihood of serious adverse effects.
Class III: Product is not likely to cause adverse effects.

Recall Process

1. There are enough adverse effects or misbranding reports that the FDA decides to recall the drug.
2. If manufacturer agrees to the recall, it works with the FDA to establish a recall strategy.
3. The manufacturer contacts customers by telegram, mailgram, or first-class letters with the following information:
    a. Product name, size, lot number, code or serial number, and other identifying information.
    b. Reason for recall and hazard involved.
    c. Instructions on what to do with the product
4. Recalls are listed in the weekly FDA Enforcement Report

FDA Market Recalls

FDA Market recalls are used to warn manufacturers to fix minor violations or remove the drugs from the market.

FDA Medical Device Safety Alerts

Medical Device Safety Alerts are used to recall medical devices.

Infection Control Standards

To prevent and control infections and contamination:

- Employees should wash their hands before and after patient interactions, before aseptic procedures, and upon contact with blood or other infectious agents.
- Equipment should be cleaned and disinfected before and after use.
- Counting trays and spatulas must be disinfected using 70% isopropyl alcohol.
- Antibiotics, and other agents that have allergy potential, should be prepared using designated and labeled trays, spatulas, etc.

Laminar Air Flow

- Biological Safety Cabinets (BSC) or Laminar Flow Hoods should be used during the preparation of hazardous materials
- BSCs should be vented to the outside
- BSCs should be cleaned before and after batch preparations
- Horizontal BSCs should not be used when preparing hazardous drugs because they increase the chance of exposure
- Hazardous material should not be stocked or worked with in an area with positive pressure relative to the surrounding area so that it does not spread.

United States Pharmacopeia and National Formulary (USP-NF)

The USP-NF sets standards for medications, dietary supplements, and food products.

USP-795

Compounding medications allows pharmacists to tailor therapy for patients that, for various reasons, may not be able to take commercially formulated drugs. USP-795 provides standards for compounding non-sterile drugs to reduce risk of contamination or incorrect dosing.

USP-797

USP-797 provides standards for compounding **sterile** drugs to reduce risk of contamination or incorrect dosing. Medications that are required to be sterile include those administered through injection, intravenous infusion (IV), intraocular (injection in the eye) or intrathecal (injection in the spine).

Hazardous Substances

Material Safety Data Sheets (MSDS)

Occupational Safety and Health Administration (OSHA) requires every pharmacy to have a Material Safety Data Sheets (MSDS) book. The MSDS contains information on chemicals, their identifying characteristics, flammability, volatility, and what to do in case of a spill or an emergency.

Storage, Handling, and Disposal

There are a lot of hazardous substances and hazardous waste found in a pharmacy. Examples of hazardous waste include expired medications, incorrectly compounded medications, bodily fluids, etc.

Hazardous waste must be put in designated bins and labeled as hazardous or biohazards. Pharmacies typically hire specialized companies to come pick up hazardous waste.

Hazardous Substance Exposure: Prevention and Treatment

OSHA requires employees to protect themselves when working with hazardous substances by wearing personal protective equipments such as gloves, gowns, goggles, feet/hair covers, and masks. Masks are used to prevent accidental ingestion and inhalation.

Skin Exposure

Skin exposure to hazardous materials can result in burns, blisters, reddening, rashes, sores, etc. If your skin comes into contact with a chemical or hazardous substance, you must notify a supervisor immediately and flush the skin with cool water for 15 minutes; remove necessary clothing before flushing your skin with water. Major burns require emergency medical help.

Eye Exposure

If your eyes come into contact with chemical or hazardous substance, have someone call for emergency medical help and remove contacts, if any, and flush your eyes at an eye wash station for 15 minutes.

Accidental Ingestion

If you accidentally ingest a chemical or hazardous substance, notify a supervisor immediately and have someone call for emergency medical help. Check the MSDS sheets for what treatment to provide and whether or not vomiting should be induced. Vomiting should not be induced if the substance is corrosive or the person is unconscious.

Inhalation

If a person has inhaled a chemical or hazardous substance, call for emergency help and move the person into an area with fresh air.

Spill Kits

Every pharmacy should have a spill kit to be used for small and medium spills; if a large spill occurs, outside may need to be called in. When a spill occurs:
1. Notify everyone in the area and evacuate, if necessary.
2. Check the MSDS for what personal protective equipment is needed and the flammability/volatility of the spilt chemical.
3. For small or medium spills, use the absorption spill kit to absorb the chemicals. For large pills, call for help.
4. After the chemicals have been absorbed, placed it in chemical spill bags for disposal.
5. Wash the area with water and detergent.
6. Notify the supervisor that a spill has occurred.

Record Keeping for Repackaged and Recalled Products and Supplies

Record Keeping for Repackaged Products

A repackaging log should be maintained for all repackaged items so that if the pharmacy receives new information about a drug, it will know which medication the new information pertains to. The repackaging log must include the following information: repackaging date, drug's name, drug's strength, dosage form, manufacturer's name, lot number, manufacturer's expiration date, beyond use date, repackaged quantity, technician's initials, pharmacist initials, prescriber's name. Drugs that are repackaged must have the following on the label: generic drug name, drug strength, dosage form, manufacturer name and lot number, expiration date. It is extremely important to record the manufacturer name and lot number for recall and quality assurance purposes.

Record Keeping for Recalled Products and Supplies

The following information must be recorded and maintained for all recalled drugs and supplies:
- Date product was removed from inventory
- Name, strength, dosage form, and quantity of drug removed
- Manufacturer and lot number
- Reason drug was removed
- Initials of technician and supervising pharmacist

Professional Standards

Pharmacy Technicians

Pharmacy technicians work under the supervision of a pharmacist. Most states limit the number of technicians a pharmacist can supervise at one time.

Pharmacy technicians should never provide medical advice; however, some of their responsibilities include the following:
- Take prescription orders from patients and check them out at the cash register.
- Viewing/entering patient data, prescription orders, and insurance information into the pharmacy software system.
- Counting or measuring drugs for a prescription order.
- Managing inventory.
- Loading drug dispensing devices at hospitals.
- Distributing medications at a hospital.
- Making IV and other sterile mixtures.

Board of Pharmacy

The Board of Pharmacy is part of the state's Department of Health. It is responsible for inspecting pharmacies and ensuring that they comply with standards and the law.

Facility, Equipment, and Supply Requirements

The State Board of Pharmacy provides guidelines on the amount of space and types of equipments needed in a pharmacy. Pharmacies must have some type of security and monitoring system to secure and watch areas where medicine is stored, counted, or dispensed. The ability to lock Schedule II substances is also required.

Pharmacies must have medication specific refrigerators and freezers. A designated compounding area with a laminar hood is required if compounding sterile medication is to be performed.

The following reference material should be available in every pharmacy:
- *Approved Drug Products with Therapeutic Equivalence and Evaluations* (a.k.a - *Orange Book*). The *Orange Book* contains information on the safety and efficacy of all FDA approved products.

Other reference materials:
- *Drug Facts and Comparisons* contains information on prescription and OTC drugs. Drugs are classified by therapeutic or pharmacological groups. It provides treatment guidelines as well as manufacturer information.
- *Physician's Desk Reference* is a compilation of medication package inserts and is updated every year.

Pharmacy Math

Roman Numerals

In the Roman Numeral system, numbers are represented by letters.

Roman Numeral	Value
ss	1/2
I	1
V	5
X	10
L	50
C	100
D	500
M	1000

Rules for writing and interpreting roman numerals:
1. When a larger numeral is followed by an equal or smaller numeral, the values are added together. For example: XI = (10 + 1) = 11.
2. When a smaller numeral is followed by a larger number, the smaller number is subtracted from the larger numeral. For example: IX = (10 - 1) = 9.
   a. I may only be subtracted from V or X
   b. X may only be subtracted from L or C
   c. C may only be subtracted from D or M
3. When a smaller numeral is between two larger numerals, subtract first and then add. For example: XXIX = XX + (10-1) = XX + 9 = 10 +10 +9 = 29.
4. Roman numerals cannot be repeated more than 3 times. For example: you cannot write 40 as XXXX. To write 40, you would use XL (50 -10) = 40.
5. V can never be repeated. For example, you can never write VV, VVX, XVV, or XVVI.

Fractions

A fraction represents a part of a whole. It has 2 parts, the numerator and the denominator. The numerator is the number above the bar and the denominator is the number below the bar. The denominator can never be 0.

Adding and Subtracting Fractions

In order to add or subtract fractions, the fractions have to have the same denominator. To find a common denominator, find the smallest multiple of both denominators or multiply the two denominators. Once you have the common denominator, you'll need to convert the fractions to their equivalent fractions. Once the fractions have the same or common denominator, add or subtract the numerators and write the result over the common denominator. Reduce the fraction result if needed. See examples below.

Example 1:

1. $\frac{1}{4} + \frac{1}{6} = ?$

2. To find the common denominator, multiply the two denominators: 4 * 6 = 24

3. To convert the fractions to their equivalents:

    a. $\frac{1}{4} = \frac{(1 * 6)}{(4 * 6)} = \frac{6}{24}$

    b. $\frac{1}{6} = \frac{(1 * 4)}{(6 * 4)} = \frac{4}{24}$

4. Now that the fractions have the same denominator, we can add them.

    a. $\frac{(4 + 6)}{24} = \frac{10}{24}$

5. Reduce the fraction. To reduce a fraction, divide the numerator and denominator by the largest common multiple.

    a. $\frac{(10 \% 2)}{(24 \% 2)} = \frac{5}{12}$

Example 2:

1. $\frac{1}{3} + \frac{3}{4} = ?$

2. Common denominator = 3 * 4 = 12

3. Equivalent fractions:

    a. $\frac{1}{3} = \frac{(1 * 4)}{(3 * 4)} = \frac{4}{12}$

    b. $\frac{3}{4} = \frac{(3 * 3)}{(4 * 3)} = \frac{9}{12}$

4. Add the fractions:

    a. $\frac{(4 + 9)}{12} = \frac{13}{12}$

5. $\frac{13}{12}$ does not have a common multiple, so cannot be reduced further.

Multiplying and Dividing Fractions

When you see the word "of" in a problem, that usually means multiplication is needed. For example, $\frac{1}{4}$ of 20 means you should multiply 20 by $\frac{1}{4}$.

To multiply fractions, multiply the two numerators to get the new numerator and multiple the two denominators to get the new denominator. Reduce the new fraction as needed. See examples below.

Example 1:

1. $\frac{1}{4} * \frac{2}{5} = ?$

2. Multiply the two numerators and then multiply the two denominators:

   a. $\frac{(1*2)}{(4*5)} = \frac{2}{20}$

3. Reduce as necessary. $\frac{2}{20}$ reduces to $\frac{1}{10}$.

Example 2:

1. $\frac{1}{10} * 20 = ?$

2. Since 20 is a whole number, use 1 as the denominator.

   a. $\frac{1}{10} * \frac{20}{1} = ?$

3. Multiply the two numerators and the two denominators:

   a. $\frac{(1*20)}{(10*1)} = \frac{20}{10}$

4. Reduce as necessary. $\frac{20}{10}$ reduces to 2.

To divide fractions, multiply the first fraction by the reciprocal (switch the numerator and denominator) of the second fraction. See examples below.

Example 1:

1. $\frac{1}{2} \% \frac{3}{5} = ?$

2. Multiply the first fraction by the reciprocal of the second fraction.

   a. $\frac{1}{2} * \frac{5}{3} = \frac{(1*5)}{(2*3)} = \frac{5}{6}$

3. Reduce as necessary. $\frac{5}{6}$ cannot be reduced any further.

Converting Fractions Into Decimals

Fractions can be converted into decimals by dividing the numerator by the denominator. For example:

1. $\frac{1}{2}$ = 1 % 2 = 0.5

2. $\frac{3}{4}$ = 3 % 4 = 0.75

Decimals

Adding and Subtracting Decimals

When adding or subtracting decimals, align the decimal points so that similar place values are aligned (i.e. the ones place in both numbers should line up, the tens place should line up, etc.) before adding or subtracting. You may add 0s to the beginning or end of a number to help line up the numbers.

Example 1:
Add 1.11 + 1.1

```
    1.11
  +1.10
  --------
    2.11
```

Example 2:
Add 1.11 + 2

```
    1.11
  +2.00
  --------
    3.11
```

Example 3:
Add 1. 11 + .5

```
    1.11
  +0.50
  --------
    1.61
```

Multiplying Decimals

To multiply decimals, multiply the numbers as if there were no decimals. Then place the decimal point, starting at the right, a number of places equal to the total number of the decimal places in both numbers.

Example 1:

Multiply 2.45 * 3.4

1. 245 * 34 = 8330
2. 2.45 has 2 decimal places and 3.4 has 1 decimal place, so there is a total of 3 decimal places
3. Place decimal point, starting at right, equal to total number of decimal places
   a. 8330 = 8.330

Converting Between Decimals and Percents

To convert from decimals to percents, move the decimal point two places to the right and add a % sign.

Example:

0.15 = 15%

To convert from percents to decimals, move the decimal point two places to the left and remove the % sign.

Example:

45% = 0.45

Measurement System

There are various systems of measurement such as metric, apothecary, household, and avoirdupois. The metric system is the most used system of measurement in pharmacy. You will need to know how to convert one unit of measurement to another. You will need to memorize common units of measurements and conversion factors.

Some common unit prefixes are:

Prefix	Symbol	Value
nano	n	0.0000000001
micro	u	0.0000001
milli	m	0.0001

centi	c	0.01
deci	d	0.1
deca	da	10
hecto	h	100
kilo	k	1,000
mega	M	1,000,000
giga	G	1,000,000,000
tera	T	1,000,000,000,000

Metric System

Liquids and lotions are measured by volume; typically, liters or milliliters. Solids such as pills, granules, ointments, etc. are measured by weight; typically, grams or milligrams.

Avoirdupois System

The avoirdupois system is a measurement system of weights which uses pounds and ounces as units. Another avoirdupois unit used in pharmacy is called the grain. 1 grain is equal to 64.8 milligrams.

Apothecary System

The apothecary system is a measurement system of mass and volume which uses ounce, pint, quart, and gallon as units. The apothecary system is not often used in pharmacy.

Household Units

Household units that are often used in liquid prescriptions include teaspoon, tablespoon, and cup.

Temperature

Celsius is the preferred unit of measurement for temperatures in pharmacy.
To convert Celsius to Fahrenheit:

Fahrenheit = ((9/5) * degrees Celsius) + 32

Example:

10 degrees Celsius = ? degrees Fahrenheit
((9/5) * 10) + 32 = (18) + 32 = 50 degrees Fahrenheit

To convert Fahrenheit to Celsius:

Celsius = (5/9) * (degrees Fahrenheit - 32)

Example:
    80 degrees Fahrenheit = ? degrees Celsius
    (5/9) * (80 - 32) = (5/9) * (48) = 26.7 degrees Celsius

Conversions

You will need to know conversion factors to convert between one unit of measure to another.

Common conversion factors are:
- 1 lb = 16 oz. or 453.59 g
- 1 oz = 437.5 gr or 28.35 g
- 1 gr = 64.8 mg
- 1 gal = 4 qt
- 1 qt = 2 pt
- 1 pt = 16 fl oz. or 473.167 mL
- 1 tsp = 5 mL
- 1 tbsp = 3 tsp = 15 mL
- 1 cup = 8 fl oz.
- 1 L = 33.8 oz
- 1 fl oz = 29.57 mL
- 1 kg = 2.2 lb

Dimensional Analysis (Factor/Label Method)

Dimensional analysis is used to solve pharmacy problems by multiplying fractions to cancel out units to get the desired units in the numerator.

Converting mL to Fluid Ounces

Question: You have a prescription for 100 mL of codeine liquid and need to know how many fluid ounces that is.
1. Find the conversion factor for mL to fluid ounces:
   a. 1 fluid ounce = 29.57 mL
2. Since the desired unit is fluid ounces, remember to keep the fluid ounces in the numerator.
3. Set up the equation to cancel out mL:

$$\frac{100\ mL}{1} \quad \times \quad \frac{1\ fluid\ ounce}{29.57\ mL} \quad = \quad \frac{100\ fluid\ ounce}{29.57} \quad = 3.38\ fluid\ ounce$$

Filling a tablet prescription

Question: You need to give a patient 700 mg of Tylenol and you only have 350 mg Tylenol tablets. How many tablets should you give the patient?

1. Find the conversion factor:
   a. 1 tablet = 350 mg
2. Since the desired unit is tablets, remember to keep tablet in the numerator.
3. Set up the equation to cancel out mg:

$$\frac{700\ mg}{1} \times \frac{1\ tablet}{350\ mg} = \frac{700\ tablets}{350} = 2\ tablets$$

Preparing IV Solutions

The concentration of electrolytes is expressed as milliequivalents (mEq) per mL.

Question: The pharmacy has Sodium Chloride 20 mEq/10 mL available. How many mL should you add to the IV if the IV should have 40 mEq of Sodium Chloride in it?
1. Since the desired units is mL, remember to keep mL in the numerator.
2. Set up the equation to cancel out mEq:

$$\frac{40\ mEq}{1} \times \frac{10\ mL}{20\ mEq} = \frac{400\ mL}{20} = 20\ mL$$

Ratios and Proportions

A ratio is a relationship between two numbers indicating how many of one thing exists in relation to another. For example, if you have 3 females for every 1 male, the female to male ratio is 3 to 1 or (3:1). You can write ratios as fractions expressed as a part to a whole. In the example above, you have 3 females to 1 male, so a total of 4 people; so ¾ are females and ¼ are males.

Proportions are equations that states that 2 ratios are equal. They are usually written as two fractions like below:

$$\frac{a}{b} = \frac{c}{d}$$

When solving problems using proportions, keep in mind the following rules:
1. Numerators must have the same units.
2. Denominators must have the same units.
3. 3 of the 4 values in the proportion must be known.

To solve proportion problems, you need to cross multiply and solve for the missing variable using algebra. Cross multiply means to multiple the numerator of each fraction with the denominator of the other fraction. See below:

$$\frac{a}{b} = \frac{c}{d} \longrightarrow ad = cb$$

Tablet Prescriptions

Question: A prescription reads amoxicillin, one tablet twice a day for 7 days. How many tablets are needed to fill the prescription?

1. The patient needs a total of 2 tablets per day. We need to figure out how many tablets in 7 days equals the same ratio as 2 tablets per day. Set up the proportion:

$$\frac{X \; tablets}{7 \; days} = \frac{2 \; tablets}{1 \; day}$$

2. Cross multiply and solve for X:

$$X \; tablet = \frac{2 \; tablets * 7 \; days}{1 \; days} = 14 \; tablets$$

Liquid Prescriptions

Question: You receive a prescription for penicillin 50 mg 3 times a day for 7 days. The pharmacy has 200 mg/5mL 100mL available. How many mL should a single dose be?

1. The problem states that there is 200mg of penicillin for every 5mL. We need figure out how many mL of the solution we need, to get 50 mg of penicillin, given that the solution has a ratio of 200 mg of penicillin per 5 mL. Set up the proportion:

$$\frac{X \; mL}{50 \; mg} = \frac{5 \; mL}{200 \; mg}$$

2. Cross multiply and solve for X:

$$X \; mL = \frac{5 \; mL * 50 \; mg}{200 \; mg} = 1.25 \; mL$$

Mixtures

Question: A mixture contains 5 mL of Lomotil in 25 mL of mixture. How many mL of Lomotil are there in a tablespoon of the mixture?

1. Find conversion factor for tablespoon to mL: 1 tablespoon = 15 mL

2. We need to figure out how many mL of Lomotil are in 15 mL (a tablespoon) of the mixture given that the ratio is 5 mL of Lomotil per 25 mL of mixture. Set up the proportion:

$$\frac{X\ mL}{15\ mL} = \frac{5\ mL}{25\ mL}$$

3. Cross multiply and solve for x:

$$X\ mL = \frac{5\ mL * 15\ mL}{25\ mL} = 3\ mL$$

Days Supply

A prescriptions reads: Tylenol 200 mg, #32, 2 capsule orally, 2 times a day. What is the days supply (how many days should the prescription last)?
  1. Find the conversion factors:
      a. 2 capsule / 1 dose (2 capsules per dose)
      b. 2 doses / 1 day (take 2 doses a day)
      c. 32 capsules
  2. Since day is the desired unit, remember to keep it in the numerator.
  3. Set up the equations to cancel out everything except days.

$$\frac{1\ day}{2\ doses}\ \text{x}\ \frac{1\ dose}{2\ capsules}\ \text{x}\ \frac{32\ capsules}{1} = \frac{32\ days}{4} = 8\ days$$

A prescription reads: Tylenol 200 mg/5 mL, #8 oz, 1 tsp, 2 times a day. What is the days supply?
  1. Convert oz to mL.

$$\frac{X\ mL}{8\ oz.} = \frac{30\ mL}{1\ oz}$$

Cross multiply and solve for X. X = 240 mL

2. Find quantity to be taken in one day
    Take 1 tsp. twice a day
    1 tsp = 5 mL
    5 mL x 2 = 10 mL a day

3. Find days supply given the ratio of taking 10 mL (1 tsp. twice a day) a day.
    $$\frac{X\ days}{240\ mL} = \frac{1\ day}{10\ mL}$$

    Cross multiply and solve for X. X = 24 days

A prescription for eye drops reads: 2 gtts, BID x 5 days # 10 mL. What is the days supply?

1. Find the number of drops in a bottle. The conversion factor is 15 gtts/mL.

$$\frac{X\ gtt}{10\ mL} = \frac{15\ gtt}{1\ mL}$$

Cross multiply and solve for X. X = 150 gtt

2. Find number of drops used in a day.
   The patient will use 2 gtts 5 times a day so, 10 gtts in a day.

3. Find the days supply given the ratio that the patient will use 10 gtts per day.

$$\frac{1\ day}{10\ gtt} = \frac{X\ days}{180\ gtt}$$

Cross multiply and solve for X. X = 18 days

IV Flow Rates and Drip Rates

The IV flow rate is the amount of IV solution administered over a period of time. The flow rate is typically expressed in mL/hour, but when using pumps to give IV fluids, the flow rate may be expressed in mL/min. Drip rates are expressed as drops per minute (gtts/min).

Flow rates can be calculated by dividing the amount of IV solution by hours or minutes:

$$Flow\ rate = \frac{mL\ of\ IV\ solutions}{(hours\ or\ minutes)}$$

Knowing the flow rate is important because it allows you to calculate the amount of IV solution needed for an order. For example, if an IV solution is being infused at a rate of 25 mL/hour, how many mL of IV solution would you need to last 8 hours?

$$\frac{8\ hours}{1}\ x\ \frac{25\ mL}{1\ hour} = 8\ x\ 25\ mL = 200\ mL$$

To calculate the drip rate based on a flow rate, use the following formula:

$$gtts/min = \frac{mL}{time\ in\ minutes}\ x\ (gtts/mL\ of\ IV\ tubing)$$

Question: An IV solution has a flow rate of 150 mL/hour and is running through 10 gtts/mL tubing. What is the drip rate?

$$gtts/min = \frac{150\ mL}{60\ minutes}\ *\ 10 = 25\ gtts/min$$

Concentration/Percent Solution

Concentration is the amount of a substance in a volume. Concentrations are expressed as weight to volume (g/100mL) or volume to volume (mL/100mL) or weight to weight (g/100g).

IV Solutions

Question: How many grams of dextrose is there in a 500 mL IV bag containing a 25% dextrose solution?

1. 25% dextrose concentration means that there are 25g of dextrose in 100 mL of solution.
2. Set up the proportion:

$$\frac{X\,g}{500\,mL} = \frac{25\,g}{100\,mL}$$

3. Cross multiply and solve for x.

$$X\,g = \frac{25g * 500\,mL}{100\,mL} = 125\,g$$

Dilutions

Dilution involves decreasing the concentration of a solution by increasing the volume. The formula for dilutions is:

   C1 * V1 = C2 * V2

C1 = concentration of stock solution you have
V1 = volume of stock solution you need to create desired solution
C2 = concentration desired or concentration of new solution
V2 = volume prescribed or final volume of new solution

Question: A patient is prescribed a 25% solution of dextrose 500 mL. You have a 50% solution of dextrose 500 mL. How do you create the prescribed solution?
C1 = concentration of stock solution you have = 50%
V1 = volume of stock solution you need = ?
C2 = concentration desired = 25%
V2 = volume prescribed or final volume of new solution = 500 mL

1. (50)(X) = (25)(500)
2. X = $\frac{25 * 500}{50}$ = 250 mL
3. You need 250 mL of the 50% solution. Since the final volume is 500 mL, you will need to add 250mL (500 - 250) of water to 250 mL of 50% solution to get 25% solution of dextrose 500 mL.

Question: You have 50 mL of a 5% solution. You add 25 mL of water to the solution. What is the concentration of the new solution?

C1 = concentration of stock solution = 5%

V1 = volume of stock solution you have = 50 mL

C2 = concentration of new solution = ?

V2 = final volume of new solution = 50 mL + 25 mL = 75 mL

1. (50) (5) = (X)(75)
2. $X = \dfrac{50 * 5}{75} = 3.3\ \%$

Question: You have a TPN order of Freamine 4%, Dextrose 30%, NaCl 20 mEq with total volume of 500 mL. You have the following in stock: Freamine 10% , Dextrose 60%, and NaCl 4 mEq/mL. How do you create the prescribed solution?
  1. Use C1V1 = C2V2 to figure out the volume of Freamine needed.
      a. (10)(x) = (4)(500)
      b. X = 200 mL of Freamine needed
  2. Use C1V1 = C2V2 to figure out the volume of Dextrose needed.
      a. (60)(X) = (30)(500)
      b. X = 250 mL of Dextrose needed
  3. Use proportions to figure out the volume of NaCl needed.
      a. $\dfrac{X\ mL}{20\ mEq} = \dfrac{1\ mL}{4\ mEq}$

      b. $X = \dfrac{(20 * 1)}{4} = 5$ mL

  4. Figure out the amount of water needed.
      a. We want a total volume of 500 mL. We have 200 mL of freamine + 250 mL of dextrose + 5 mL of NaCl = 455 mL.
      B. We need 45 mL (500 - 455) of water.

Alligation

Alligation, also called the Tic-Tac-Toe method, is used when preparing mixtures of two different concentrations of the same ingredient to get a different concentration.

Higher % concentration		Desired % concentration minus lower % concentration. (let's call this box A)
	Desired % concentration	
Lower % concentration		Higher % concentration

		minus desired % concentration (let's call this box B)

Alligation Steps:
1. Fill in the boxes.
2. Add box A and box B to get the Total Parts.
3. To find the relative amount of the higher % concentration to use, divide Box A by the Total Parts.
4. To find the relative amount of the lower % concentration to use, divide Box B by the Total Parts.

Question: How many grams of 2% bacitracin should be mixed with 5% bacitracin to get 20 grams of 3% bacitracin ointment?

5		1
	3	
2		2

Total Parts : 1 + 2 = 3
Relative amount of higher % concentration to use: 1 / 3
Relative amount of lower % concentration to use: 2 /3
Grams of 5% bacitracin needed = total grams desired * relative amount of higher %
$$= 20g * (\tfrac{1}{3}) = 6.7g$$
Grams of 2% bacitracin needed = total grams desired * relative mount of lower %
$$= 20g * (\tfrac{2}{3}) = 13.3g$$

Powder Volume

Powder volume is the space occupied by the powder after it is dissolved or dispersed in liquid. Powder volume calculations are used to determine the concentration of a medicine after diluent is added or to calculate the amount of diluent needed to obtain a certain concentration. The formula is as follows:

FV = final volume of constituted product
D = volume of diluent
PV = powder volume
$$FV = D + PV$$

Question: A bottle of Amoxicillin 250 mg/5ml for oral suspension requires the addition of 70 mL of water to give a 150 mL suspension. What is the total diluent volume needed to obtain a concentration of 165 mg/5 ml?

1. Determine the total mg of drugs in the bottle:

    a. $\dfrac{250\ mg}{5\ mL}$ * 150 mL = 7,500 mg

2. Find the powder volume for the drugs in the bottle:

    a. FV = D + PV

    b. 150 mL = 70 mL + PV

    c. PV = 80 mL

3. Find what the final volume of the produce should be to obtain a concentration of 165 mg/5ml:

    a. $\dfrac{7500\ mg}{X\ mL} = \dfrac{165\ mg}{5\ mL}$

    b. Cross multiply and solve for X.

    c. X = 227.3 mL

4. Find the total amount of diluent needed:

    a. FV = D + PV

    b. 227.3 mL = D + 80 mL

    b. total amount of diluent needed is 147.3 mL

Dosing

Pediatric Dosage Calculations

Follow manufacturer provided dosage instructions if provided. If children's dosage are not provided, there are a few methods you can use to calculate the dosage for a child.

Clark's Rule

Child dose = $\dfrac{weight\ of\ child\ in\ lbs}{150\ lbs}$ * adult dose

Young's Rule

Child dose = $\dfrac{age\ of\ child}{age\ of\ child + 12}$ * adult dose

Body Surface Area (BSA) Formula

Child dose = $\dfrac{child\ BSA}{average\ adult\ BSA}$ * adult dose

The BSA is based on the height and weight of an individual and is always expressed in square meters. The average adult BSA is 1.73 square meters. You can calculate an individual's BSA using a nomogram or a computer program. To find the BSA using a nomogram, draw a line between the height and weight; the point of intersection on the BSA column is the BSA for the corresponding height and weight.

Question: If the adult dose of a drug is 250 mg, what is the dose for a child weighing 75 lbs?

1. Child Dose = $\dfrac{75\ lbs}{150\ lbs}$ * 250 mg = 125 mg

Question: If the adult dose of a drug is 250 mg, what is the does for a child that is 10 years old?

1. Child Dose = $\dfrac{10}{10 + 12}$ * 250 mg = 113.6 mg

Geriatric Dosage

Geriatric patients are those who are 65 years or older. As our body ages, our ability to absorb, distribute, metabolize, and excrete (ADME) changes; this may require changes to the dosage of certain drugs. The Geriatric Dosage Handbook should be consulted when calculating dosages for geriatric patients.

Practice Questions

1. How do you write 49 in roman numeral?
   a. IL
   b. XLIX
   c. XXXXIX
   d. XXXXIVIIII

2. How many tsps equal 30 mLs?
   a. 2 tsps
   b. 3 tsps
   c. 6 tsps
   d. 8 tsps

3. A doctor orders DrugA 50mg/mL for a patient at 1 mL every 12 hours for 5 days. What is the total volume to be dispensed, in mL, if the only DrugA stock you have is 100mg/5mL?
   a. 10 mL
   b. 25 mL
   c. 50 mL
   d. 75 mL

4. You need to make a hydrocortisone 20% cream. How many grams of hydrocortisone is needed to make 50 grams of the cream.
   a. 10 g
   b. 20 g
   c. 25 g
   d. 30 g

5. A doctor prescribes Tylenol 200 mg, #24, 2 capsule orally, 3 times a day. What is the days supply?
   a. 4 days
   b. 6 days
   c. 8 days
   d. 12 days

6. The flow rate of an IV solution is 100 mL/hour. How long will a 1500 mL IV bag last?
   a. 10 hours
   b. 15 hours
   c. 20 hours
   d. 30 hours

7. A patient is prescribed a 20% solution of dextrose 250 mL. You have a 50% stock solution of dextrose 500 mL. How many mL of of the stock solution is needed?
   a. 50
   b. 75
   c. 100
   d. 150

8. According to Clark's Rule, if the adult dose of a drug is 250 mg, what is the dose for a 8 year old that weighs 75 lbs?
   a. 100 mg
   b. 115 mg
   c. 125 mg
   d. 150 mg

9. How many grams of 5% bacitracin should be mixed with 10% bacitracin to get 20 grams of 7% bacitracin ointment?
   a. 8 g
   b. 10 g
   c. 12 g
   d. 14 g

10. How many grams of dextrose should be added to 200 mL to obtain a 35% dextrose solution?
    a. 35 g

b. 70 g

c. 75 g

d. 100 g

Practice Question Answers

1. B. 49 in Roman numerals is XLIX. It cannot be IL because only X can be subtracted from L or C. It can't be XXXXIX or XXXXIVIIII because roman numerals cannot be repeated more than 3 times.

2. C. 6 tsps equals 30 mLs.

   a. 1 tsp = 5 mL

   $$\frac{30\ mL}{1} \ \mathbf{X}\ \frac{1\ tsp}{5mL} = 6\ tsp.$$

3. D. First, figure out how many mL total is prescribed for 5 days.

   $$\frac{1\ mL}{12\ hours} \ \mathbf{X}\ \frac{24\ hours}{1\ day} \ \mathbf{X}\ \frac{5\ days}{1} = 10\ mL$$

   Then, figure out how many total mg of DrugA was prescribed.

   $$\frac{50\ mg}{mL} \ \mathbf{X}\ \frac{10\ mL}{1} = 500\ mg$$

   Then, figure out how many mL of the stock solution would give us 500 mg.

   $$\frac{5mL}{100mg} \ \mathbf{X}\ \frac{500\ mg}{1} = 25\ mL$$

4. A. First, we need to set up the proportion. 20% means 20g/100g and we need to make 50 grams of the cream, so we need to figure out how many grams of hydrocortisone will be needed in a 50 gram cream to equal 20% or 20g/100g.

   $$\frac{20g}{100g} = \frac{X}{50g}$$

   Then, cross multiply and solve for X.

   X = 10 g

5. A. First, we need to figure out how many pills are prescribed for a day.

   $$\frac{2\ capsules}{1\ dose} \ \mathbf{X}\ \frac{3\ doses}{1\ day} = \frac{6\ capsules}{1\ day}$$

   Then, we need to figure out how many days 24 capsules will last.

   $$24\ capsules\ \mathbf{X}\ \frac{1\ day}{6\ capsules} = 4\ days$$

6. B. Use the following IV Flow Rate formula and solve for time:

$$\text{Flow rate} = \frac{mL \ of \ Solution}{time \ in \ hours}$$

$$\frac{100 \ mL}{hour} = \frac{1500 \ mL}{X}$$

X = 15 hours

7. C. Use the formula for dilutions: C1 * V1 = C2 * V2
   C1 = concentration of stock solution you have = 50%
   V1 = volume of stock solution you need = ?
   C2 = concentration desired = 20%
   V2 = volume prescribed or final volume of new solution = 250 mL
   (50)(X) = (20)(250)
   X = 100 mL of stock solution needed.

8. C. Clark's rule formula is:

$$\text{Child dose} = \frac{weight \ of \ child \ in \ lbs}{150 \ lbs} * \text{adult dose}$$

$$\text{Child dose} = \frac{75 \ lbs}{150 \ lbs} \text{ X 250 mg = 125 mg}$$

9. C. 12 g of 5% bacitracin is needed.

Higher % concentration		Desired % concentration minus lower % concentration. (let's call this box A)
	Desired % concentration	
Lower % concentration		Higher % concentration minus desired % concentration (let's call this box B)

Alligation Steps:
1. Fill in the boxes.
2. Add box A and box B to get the Total Parts.
3. To find the relative amount of the higher % concentration to use, divide Box A by the Total Parts.

4. To find the relative amount of the lower % concentration to use, divide Box B by the Total Parts.

10		(7 - 5) = 2
	7	
5		(10 -7) = 3

Total Parts : 2 + 3 = 5

Relative amount of higher % concentration to use: 2 / 5

Relative amount of lower % concentration to use: 3 / 5

Grams of 10% bacitracin needed = total grams desired * relative amount of higher %

$$= 20g * (2/5) = 8 \text{ g}$$

Grams of 5% bacitracin needed = total grams desired * relative mount of lower %

$$= 20g * (3/5) = 12 \text{ g}$$

10. B. 70 grams of dextrose should be added to 200 mL to get a 35% dextrose solution.

   1. 35% dextrose concentration means that there are 35 g of dextrose in 100 mL of solution.

   2. Set up the proportion:

$$\frac{X \, g}{200 \, mL} = \frac{35 \, g}{100 \, mL}$$

   3. Cross multiply and solve for x. X = 70 g.

Sterile and Non-Sterile Compounding

Compounding, the process of mixing and preparing drugs, allows pharmacists to tailor therapy for patients that may not be able to take commercially formulated drugs. Some reasons for compounding include adjusting a dose, flavoring medication, removing an ingredient a patient is allergic to, or changing the dosage form of a medication. Sterile compounding is used for drugs that are administered through injection, IV, intraocularly, or intrathecally. Non-sterile compounding is used for tablets, capsules, creams, suspensions, suppositories, and transdermal applications.

Documentation

Proper documentation for all compounded preparations should be kept so that technicians can use those records to consistently reproduce the compounded medication. Maintaining records is also important for liability reasons because they provide a way to review procedures and ingredients if there is a problem. There are 4 types of compounding records:

Record Type	Explanation
Master Formulation Record	A "recipe" for the compounded medication. It contains a list of ingredients, equipments needed, calculations used, instructions for mixing, labeling requirements, and compatibility and stability requirements.
Compounding Record	A record of what happened/results of the compounding. It contains information such as the preparer's name, master formulation record reference, products and quantities used (including those tossed out due to error), beyond use date, storage requirements, label, description of final preparation, etc.
Standard Operating Procedures	Documents the standard operating procedures for ensuring safety and quality. Includes equipment maintenance records, equipment calibration, handling and disposing of supplies,etc.
Ingredients Record	Includes Certificates of Purity and Material Safety Data Sheets.

USP 795 requires pharmacies to keep master formulation records and compounding records for all preparations, except for preparations made according to the manufacturer's labeling instructions. Records must be kept for the same amount of time as that required for the corresponding prescription.

Sterile Compounding Processes

Sterile means free from microorganisms or disease causing pathogens. Sterile compounding is used for drugs that are administered through injection, IV, intraocularly, or intrathecally. In sterile preparations, only the following types of water may be used: water for injection USP, sterile water for injection USP, and bacteriostatic water for injection USP. All sterile compounding must occur in a designated compounding area; this is also where the laminar flow workbench must be located. There should also be an anteroom, separate from the designated compounding area, used to wash hands and decontaminate supplies and equipments.

When compounding sterile solutions, solutions must be:
- Free of microorganisms and pathogens
- Free of visible contaminants
- Pyrogen (chemicals produced by microorganisms that can cause fever) free
- Stable
- Intravenous solutions should have an osmotic pressure similar to blood

Infection Control

To control contamination, aseptic techniques and environment controls must be used.

Primary Engineering Controls (PECs)

A PEC is a device or room that provides the necessary air quality for compounding sterile preparations. Sterile compounding must be prepared in an ISO Class 5 environment; this means that the area cannot have more than 100 particles per cubic foot. Common PECs include laminar airflow workstations, biological safety cabinets, compounding aseptic isolators, and compounding aseptic containment isolators.

Laminar Airflow Workstations

Laminar airflow workstations provides a work area with clean air. Air in the workstation is filtered through a high-efficiency particulate air (HEPA) filter to remove contaminants. Airflow may be horizontal or vertical. The laminar flow hood should be running continuously.

When working with laminar airflow workstations:
- Close doors or windows as breezes can interfere with the airflow enough to contaminate the area.
- All work should be done at least 6 inches inside the workstation since laminar flow air near the edge of a workstation may be contaminated. In a horizontal laminar flow hood, nothing should pass behind a sterile object.
- Do not use laminar airflow workstations to prepare chemotherapy agents or other hazardous drugs because laminar airflow workstations do not protect personnel nor the environment from hazards.

- Laminar flow hoods should be cleaned top to bottom, back to front away from the HEPA filter prior to each use.

Biological Safety Cabinets

Biological safety cabinets provide clean air as well as protect the personnel and the environment from hazardous air. They are often used for compounding hazardous substances such as chemotherapy agents. Biological safety cabinets works by filtering air using a HEPA air filter and using vents to pull air back into the cabinet to prevent hazardous air from spreading to other environments.

Biological safety cabinets should not be used for working with volatile toxic chemicals or radio-nucleotides. Volatile toxic chemicals require double HEPA filtration and radiopharmaceuticals require lead-lined walls.

Clean Rooms

Clean rooms provide an ISO Class 5 environment for the entire room. A clean room will contain a direct compounding area (DCA) where all compounding takes place. Next to the clean room is the buffer area. The **buffer area** is where components and supplies are gathered and prepared. The area directly outside the buffer area is called the anteroom. The **anteroom** is where personnel perform activities such as hand washing, garbing, label preparation, unpacking and opening or boxes, etc.

Isolators

Isolators provide an airtight glove design that lets users perform tasks inside the isolator. Compounding Aseptic Isolators (CAI) provide an aseptic environment within the isolator. Compounding Aseptic Containment Isolators (CACI) are CAIs that also protect workers from exposure to hazardous substances.

Aseptic Techniques

Aseptic techniques are methods used to minimize particle and microbial contamination.

Garbing

When compounding sterile preparations, the first thing technicians should do is remove all jewelry and put on appropriate personal protective equipments such as gloves, masks, goggles, gowns, shoe covers, hair covers, etc. You should cover up starting from the dirtiest to the cleanest part of the body (first put on shoe covers, then head/facial hair cover, then face mask, then eyeshields). After garbing, you should wash your hands.

Hand Washing Procedure

1. Stand far enough from the sink so that clothing does not touch the sink.
2. Wet hands and forearms and then apply soap.

3. Rub all areas of the hands, including under the nails and the wrists and arms up to the elbows, for 15 to 30 seconds.
4. Rinse and dry hands using a paper towel.
5. Use the paper towel to turn off the faucet.

Put on Gloves

After washing your hands, you should put on sterile gloves.
1. Spray hands with sterile 70% isopropyl alcohol and allow to dry.
2. Put on sterile gloves; gloves should cover the sleeves of the gown.
3. Spray both gloves with 70% isopropyl alcohol

Clean PEC Device Before Compounding

Before compounding, you should clean the PEC device.
1. Spray gauze pad with 70% isopropyl alcohol and use it to wipe the device. Do not reclean any previously cleaned area.
2. Use as many gauze pads (sprayed with 70% isopropyl alcohol) as necessary, using a new gauze for each surface.

Collect and Sterilize Supplies

1. Collect all supplies and check expiration dates, particulates, and leaks. Only use pre-sterilized needles, syringes, and filters.
2. Remove dust coverings before putting supplies in a PEC.
3. To maximize laminar air flow, put smaller items closer to the HEPA filter and larger items away from the HEPA filter. Large items can interfere with the airflow.
4. Use an alcohol wipe to wipe any items or surfaces that require an entry/puncture.
5. Place non-sterile objects downstream from sterile ones so that particles blown off non-sterile objects don't contaminate items downstream.

Working with Syringes and Needles

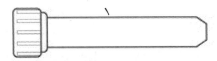

Disposable syringe and needle (parts labelled)

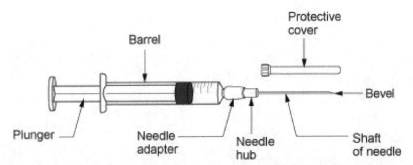

The main parts of a syringe are the barrel and plunger. There are graduation lines on the barrel to indicate the volume of liquid in the barrel. When measuring the volume of liquid in a syringe, the syringe should be held upright and all the air must be removed; measure to the edge of the plunger's stopper. When drawing liquids into the syringe, the tip of the syringe must be fully submerged to avoid drawing in air. You should draw in an excess amount of liquid which can then be expelled to get rid of air bubbles.

The main parts of a needle are the hub, shaft, and bevel. The hub is the part of the needle that attaches to the syringe. The shaft is the stem of the needle and the bevel is at the end of the shaft. The hollow bore of the shaft is called the lumen. Needles are referred to by their gauge (size of the lumen) and shaft length (measured in inches from where the shaft meets the hub to the tip of the bevel). The higher the gauge number, the smaller the lumen.

The needle size to use depends on the viscosity of the solution and the type of rubber closure in the container. The more viscous the solution, the bigger the lumen needed unless the rubber closure is of a type that can be easily cored; in which case, you should use a smaller needle regardless of the viscosity of the solution.

Transfer needles have shafts on both ends of the hub which enables the sterile transmission of liquid from one container to another without the need for a syringe.

Filter needles are needles that contain a filter that can be used to filter out particles.

For sterility reasons, disposable needles (which are presterilized and individually wrapped to ensure sterility) should always be used when preparing admixtures.

Working with Filters

There are 2 main types of filters: depth filters and membrane filters. Depth filters are a type of filter consisting of either multiple layers or a single layer of a medium having depth, which captures contaminants within its structure, as opposed to on the surface. Membrane filters catch contaminants larger than the pore size of the filter surface.

Membrane filters are often used to filter a solution as it is expelled from a syringe. Depth filters can be used to filter a solution as it is being drawn into OR expelled from a syringe, but not both ways in the same procedure.

Working with Vials

Vials are glass containers that often contain injectable medications.

When working with vials:
1. Remove vial cover and disinfect the rubber stopper using 70% isopropyl alcohol.
2. Draw a volume of air into the syringe that is equal to the volume of solution to be withdrawn.
3. Uncap the needle and insert it into the vial without coring (see section on "Preventing Coring"). Push the air from the syringe into the vial.
4. Turn the vial upside down, pull back on the plunger, and fill the syringe.
5. Remove any bubbles by tapping the syringe or pushing/pulling on the plunger.
6. Transfer solution into the desired container.

Preventing Coring

Coring is when a needle damages parts of a rubber stopper, causing pieces of rubber to contaminate the solution. To prevent coring when inserting a needle:
1. Place the vial on a flat surface and place the needle with the bevel side up at a 45 to 60 degree angle to the surface of the stopper.
2. Push down on the needle while bringing it to an upright position. By the time the needle penetrates the stopper completely, it should be at a 90 degree angle to the surface of the stopper.

Working with Ampules

Ampules are single-use, sealed glass containers that contain a neck that must be snapped off before use.
1. Wipe the neck of the ampule with 70% isopropyl alcohol.
2. Wrap the alcohol swab around the neck of the ampule to prevent glass fragments from cutting your fingers.
3. Hold the top of the ampule with your thumb and index finger. Use your other hand to hold the bottom of the ampule.
4. Snap the ampule, moving your hands out and away.

5. Hold the ampule at about a 20 degree angle and insert a 5 micron filter needle (to prevent glass contamination) into the ampule. Pull back the plunger and withdraw the solution.
6. Remove the filter needle for a new filter needle or membrane filter and transfer the solution into the desired container.

LVP/SVP Solution Bags

Parenteral means introduced by means other than through the intestinal tract such as injection, intravenous, etc. Large volume parenteral (LVP) solution bags, typically plastic, hold 100mL or more of IV solution; small volume parenteral (SVP) bags hold less than 100 mL. The bags have two ports at the bottom; the administration set port and the medication port. An administration set has an attached spike that can be used to puncture the administration set port to allow medication to flow out of the bag and into the administration set. The medication port is where drugs are added to the LVP solution using a needle and syringe.

SVP solutions can be added to LVP solutions or used as a piggyback on the LVP. When a SVP is added to a parenteral solution, the resulting solution is called an admixture. Piggybacking is when a SVP and LVP are hung together and share the same IV tubing; the SVP is attached to the injection port.

Total Parenteral Nutrition Solutions

Total Parenteral Nutrition (TPN) solutions provide patients who are unable to digest food with nutrition through an IV. TPNs consists of an amino acid solution (for protein), a dextrose solution (for carbohydrates), electrolytes, vitamins, and trace elements. When intravenous fat emulsion is added to TPNs, the resulting solution is called a total nutrient admixture (TNA).

Dialysis Solutions

Peritoneal dialysis solutions are used by patients with kidney disfunction to help remove waste. The solutions are hypertonic to blood so, through osmosis, toxic substances will move into the dialysis solution.

Irrigation Solutions

Irrigation solutions are not injected into the venous system, but must be sterile because they are used to bathe body tissues, wash instruments, and moisten dressings during surgical operations. Irrigation solutions are typically 1.5% Glycine or 3% Sorbitol; Glycine and Sorbine are used because they are non-hemolytic (they do not damage blood cells).

Non-sterile compounding processes

Non-sterile compounding preparations may contain active as well as inactive ingredients. Active ingredients cause a therapeutic response, inactive ingredients do not. Below is a table of commonly used inactive ingredients (Source: Koborsi Tadros, pg 116).

Inactive Ingredient	Description	Example
Acidifying agent	Provides acidic medium to improve stability	Citric acid, acetic acid, hydrochloric acid
Alkalizing agent	Provide alkaline medium to improve stability	Ammonia solution, ammonium carbonate, Sodium bicarbonate, potassium hydroxide
Colorants	Adds color	FD&C red
Emulsifying agents	Helps keep particles in liquid dispersed	Benzalkonium chloride glyceryl monostearate
Flavorants	Adds flavor	Cherry flavoring
Gelling agents	Used to increase viscosity	Carbopol 940
Levigating agents	Helps reduce particle size	Mineral oil, glycerin
Lubricants	Prevents ingredients from clumping	Magnesium stearate
Preservatives	Protects from microbial growth	methylparaben
Suspending agents	Helps increase viscosity to prevent settling of particles in liquid	Sodium lauryl sulfate, agar, bentonite
Sweeteners	Adds sweetness	sorbitol
Wetting agents/ Surfactants	Reduces surface tension to allow liquids to spread more easily	Betadex sulfobutyl Ether sodium Polysorbate 80

Selection and Use of Equipment and Supplies

Weighing Equipment

A balance is used to weigh powder, liquid, and other ingredients used in compounded preparations. There are 3 major types of balances: Class III torsion balances, electronic balances, and analytical balances. Analytical balances are used to weight small milligram and micrograms of material; they are typically only found in research laboratories.

Balances should always be placed on a level surface. A clean weighing paper or boat should always be used for each new ingredient to prevent cross contamination and reduce loss of drugs to porous surfaces. Use a spatula to add or remove ingredients from the balance instead of pouring it directly from the bottle. Clean the balance after use.

Volumetric Equipment

Volumetric equipment is typically used to measure and transfer liquid. Some common volumetric equipments are: pipettes, graduated cylinders, volumetric flasks, burets, and syringes. To minimize errors in measurement, always use the small equipment capable of holding the desired amount of liquid. Oily and viscous liquids are hard to remove from cylinders and pipettes so consider using a syringe instead or measuring by weight instead of volume.

Liquids have a meniscus (surface of the liquid curves downward toward the center) when they are poured into containers. Hold the container so that the meniscus is at eye level and read the graduation mark at the bottom of the meniscus.

Graduated Cylinders

Cylindrical graduates are preferred over conical graduates because they are more accurate. When selecting a graduated cylinder, choose the smallest one possible. If measuring volumes less than 20 mL, it's better to use a syringe or pipette. Amount of liquid measured should be at least 20% or more of the cylinder's capacity.

Volumetric Flasks

Volumetric flasks are used for precise dilutions. These flasks are usually pear-shaped, with a long, thin neck and bulb-like bottom. Because of the narrow neck, they are hard to use when dissolving solids in liquids.

Syringes

Syringes are useful for measuring and delivering small amounts of viscous liquids. They are especially useful for delivering oral medications.

Pipettes

Pipettes are thin tubes made of glass or plastic typically used to measure volumes less than 25 mL and are required for volumes less than 1 mL.

Single Volume Pipettes are used for transferring accurate amounts of liquid; they cannot be partially filled.

Calibrated Pipettes are like single volume pipettes except they have multiple graduation marks and can be partially filled.

Micropipettes are used to measure very small volumes, typically less than 1 mL.

Transfer Pipettes are not used to measure volume, but to transfer liquid into some other equipment when an accurate transfer amount is not required.

Mixing Solids and Semisolids

Mortars and Pestles and Sieves

Trituration is the process of grinding powders to reduce particle size. Mortars and pestles are used to triturate powders. There are 3 types of mortars and pestles: glass, Wedgewood, and porcelain. Wedgewood and porcelain mortars are used to grind large particles into powders. Glass mortars and pestles are used for mixing liquids and semi-solids. To further reduce the size of particles, powders may be passed through a sieve.

Mixing Powders

Geometric dilution is a technique used to mix two powders of unequal quantity into a homogenous mixture. First, the smaller quantity power is mixed with an equal amount of the other powder until a uniform mixture results. Then, the leftover powder is continually added in small amounts and mixed until of the powder has been used.

Spatulas

Spatulas are used to transfer solid ingredients or to mix ingredients such as ointments and creams. Iodine can corrode stainless steel, so rubber or plastic spatulas should be used when working with iodine. **Spatulation** is the technique of using a spatula to mix powders. It is often used when mixing powders that can form eutectic mixtures. Eutectic powders partially liquefy when mixed.

Ointment Slabs

Ointment slabs are hard and non-absorbable surfaces used for mixing ointments and cream.

Levigation

Levigation is a technique used to reduce particle size by triturating it with a liquid. It is generally used when preparing a drug for incorporation into a suspension, ointment, or suppository.

A hot plate is used to mix solids and semi-solids in a beaker by melting them together. The hot plate should be low temperature (25C to 120C) since most pharmaceutical solids and semi-solids melt at 70C.

Compounding Solutions

Solutions are liquids in which an active drug is dissolved. The solubility of a drug must be known before attempting to prepare a solution. To find the solubility of a drug in a solvent, see Remington: The Science and Practice of Pharmacy. Solubility is stated in terms of the volume of solvent (not volume of final solution) needed to dissolve 1 gram of the drug. Most solutions require shaking or stirring for mixing. Some solids need to be triturated before dissolving in a solution.

Non-aqueous Solutions

Non-aqueous solutions are solutions where solutes are dissolved in any solvent other than water or in addition to water. Examples of non-aqueous solutions include elixirs, tinctures, glycerates, collodions, liniments, oleaginous solutions. When compounding non-aqueous solutions, dissolve water soluble items in water and dissolve non-water soluble items in the appropriate solvent separately, before mixing the two together.

Compounding Suspensions

Suspensions consist of finely grounded solids dispersed in a liquid. Suspensions often require the addition of flocculating agents and thickening agents to control settling. **Flocculating agents** are electrolytes that help with dispersing particles or keeping particles dispersed. **Thickening agents** help keep particles from settling. Suspensions must be dispensed in bottles with enough room for shaking the suspension and with the label "Shake Well".

Below is a general outline for compounding suspensions.
1. The solid drug to be suspended is levigated with a levigating agent (e.g., mineral oil, glycerin) in a mortar.
2. A portion of the suspension vehicle, a liquid, is added to the contents of the mortar and mixed until a uniform mixture is achieved. The uniform mixture is transferred to the final container.
3. Rinse the mortar and pestle with the remaining suspension vehicle and poured into the final container until the desired volume is obtained.

Compounding Emulsions

An emulsion is a mixture of two or more liquids that are immiscible. Immiscible means it does not form a homogenous mixture when mixed together (e.g. oil and water). Emulsifiers, surfactants, or surface active ingredients are used to help stabilize emulsions (i.e., prevent components from separating). Examples of emulsifiers are sodium lauryl sulfate and sodium dioctyl sulfosuccinate. Emulsions are usually formed through shaking, heat, or trituration.

Oil in water (o/w) emulsions are when oils, petroleum hydrocarbons, and/or waxes are dispersed into a liquid. A hydrophilic emulsifier is used to stabilize o/w emulsions.

Water in oil (w/o) emulsions are when liquid is dispersed in oil. A lipophilic emulsifier is used to stabilize w/o emulsions.

The following methods are used for making emulsions: Continental (Dry Gum), Wet Gum, and Beaker.

Continental (Dry Gum) Technique

A primary emulsion is formed using 4 parts oil, 2 parts water, and 1 part gum emulsifier. The **oil and gum** are first triturated in a mortar and pestle. Then water is added to that mixture and the combined mixture is triturated until the primary emulsion is formed. Additional ingredients can be mixed in after the primary emulsion is formed.

Wet Gum Technique

A primary emulsion is formed using 4 parts oil, 2 parts water, and 1 part gum emulsifier. The **water and gum** are first triturated in a mortar and pestle to form a mucilage. Then oil is added, in portions. The mixture is triturated each time you add oil. Additional ingredients can be mixed in after the primary emulsion is formed.

Beaker Technique

The beaker technique is used to make emulsions like lotions or creams. All oil soluble ingredients are dissolved in a beaker and all water soluble ingredients are dissolved in a different beaker. Each beaker is then heated using a low-temperature hot plate or steam bath. After the beakers are removed from the heat, the internal phase (dispersed liquid) is added to the external phase (dispersion medium) with continual stirring.

Compounding Ointments

If an ointment base will be used as a drug delivery vehicle, you should choose an ointment base based upon its ability to release drugs. Water miscible or aqueous bases release drugs quickly. Oil based ointment bases generally release drugs slowly and unpredictably.

Ointments are usually compounded on an ointment slab by using geometric dilution and spatulas to combine the ingredients. Drugs in powder or crystal form need to be triturated or dissolved in solvent before being added into an ointment base.

Compounding Suppositories

There are 3 major suppository bases: oleaginous, water soluble or miscible, hydrophilic. Some examples of oleaginous bases are cocoa butter and synthetic triglycerides. Water soluble or miscible bases contain glycerinated glycerin or polyethylene glycol (PEG); glycerin and PEG dissolve slowly and provide prolonged release of active ingredients. Hydrophilic bases contain cholesterol or lanolin to help with water absorption.

Compression molding or fusion molding (the more often used method) is used to make suppositories. In compression molding, the suppository base and active ingredients are pressed into a compression mold. In fusion molding, active ingredients are dissolved in a melted suppository base and then poured into a mold.

Compounding Capsules

When compounding capsules, choose the smallest size possible as people often have difficulty swallowing large capsules. Capsules can be filled with powder or liquid. To select the correct capsule size for powders, compare the density of the powder to the density of a known drug since powders with similar density will fit into the same capsule size.

The punch method is used to fill a small number of capsules. Capsule filling machines are used when a large number of capsules need to be filled. In the punch method, the powders are triturated and then mixed. The mixture is then heaped onto an ointment slab and an empty capsule is "punched" into the heap to fill the capsule. Powder is removed/added until the correct amount has been put in the capsule. To determine whether the correct amount of drug has been placed in the capsule, weigh the capsule against an empty capsule.

To protect capsules from humidity or dryness, dispense them in plastic or glass vials and store in a cool, dry place.

Compounding Tablets

Tablets are formed by mixing active ingredients with one of the following bases: lactose, dextrose, sucrose, mannitol. The active ingredients are triturated and mixed with the tablet base; then the mixture is moistened with an alcohol and water solution so that the mixture will stick together when pressed into the tablet triturate molds. Tablet triturate molds must be calibrated each time since different combinations of drugs will have different densities.

Determine Product Stability

Stability

Stability is the ability of a drug to maintain the same characteristics and properties it had when it was made. There are 3 major causes of instability: physical, chemical, and microbiological. You can find incompatibility information in the manufacturer's package insert.

An example of a visible sign of chemical incompatibility is a change in color or the formation of a precipitate. An example of an invisible sign of chemical incompatibility is the formation of gases or of volatile chemicals.

Below are some signs of instability (Source: Pharmacy Technician, pg.276):

Dosage Form	Signs of Instability
capsules	Change in physical appearance or consistency such as hardening, softening, discoloration
powders	Caking or discoloration; uncharacteristic odor; release of pressure upon opening the container may indicate a release of carbon dioxide from bacterial or other degradation
solutions	Precipitates, discoloration, uncharacteristic odor
emulsions	Non-uniform globule size distribution and viscosity; breaking, creaming, microbial growth
suspensions	Caking, crystal growth, difficulty resuspending, non-uniform particle size
ointments	Non-uniform appearance, change in consistency, separation of liquid, grittiness, dryness
creams	Non-uniform appearance, emulsion breakage, crystal growth, discoloration
suppositories	Non-uniform appearance, softening, drying, oil stains on the packaging
gel	Non-uniform appearance, separation of liquid from gel, discoloration
IV therapy	Phase separation, turbidity, precipitates

Factors that affect stability include:
- pH - combining drugs that require different pH values can cause the drugs to degrade
- Light - some drugs break down when exposed to light
- Temperature - store drugs at proper temperature; many drugs degrade in heat

- Dilution - make sure drug is properly diluted before combining with other drugs
- Filters - filters can reduce the concentration of a drug if the drug gets trapped in the filter
- Solutions - the wrong solution or diluent can cause drugs to break down or precipitate
- Chemical complexation - when two drugs combine to form another drug, which may change the therapeutic effects of the drugs
- Plastics - some drugs bind to plastic materials (especially PVC plastics) making it unavailable for therapeutic activity

Beyond Use Date

Beyond use dates are used only for compounded preparations; they are different from expiration dates. USP-NF 795 defines the beyond use date as "the date after which a compounded preparation should not be used; determined from the date the preparation is compounded". Below is a guideline for setting beyond-use dates (Source: Pharmacy Technician, pg. 277):

1. If the preparation has an official USP-NF monograph, the beyond use date and packaging requirements are given in the monograph.
2. If there isn't an official USP-NF monograph and the compounded drug was prepared according to manufacturer's direction, beyond use dates can be set using the manufacturer's label.
3. If there isn't an official USP-NF monograph and the compounded drug was NOT prepared according to manufacturer's direction, use drug specific stability information from reference books.
4. If there are no references that evaluate the exact same formulations, use the USP-NF guidelines below:

Formulation	Maximum Beyond Use Date for Non-sterile Compounded Preparations
Oral preparations containing water	No later than 14 days stored at a controlled cold temperature
Topical, dermal, mucosal liquid and semisolid preparations containing water	No later than 30 days
Non-aqueous preparations	The earliest expiration date of any ingredient or 6 months, whichever is earlier

Final Inspection

Once compounding is complete, you should check the preparation for the following:
- There are no leaks, cracks, or leaking stoppers in containers
- Clarity, color, odor, consistency, fill volume are what is expected

- There are no unexpected precipitation, crystallization, or particulate matter
- Sterility and bacterial endotoxins testing has been done as required

You should also check that the labeling matches the prescription and check the following:
- Correct container is used.
- Label is complete and error free with storage and usage instructions and correct beyond use date.
- Correct strength and quantity of parenteral ingredients and drug additives.
- Calculated yield is consistent with actual yield.

Handling and Disposal Requirements

Pharmaceutical waste should be disposed of according to US Environmental Protection Agency (EPA) guidelines. Hazardous waste includes any used, unused, or expired drugs; partial doses in syringes; items contaminated with bodily fluids, etc.. Hazardous waste should be put in leak proof bags and clearly labeled as hazardous waste; they should also be placed in bins designated and labeled for hazardous waste. Biohazards and sharp objects like needles and syringes should be disposed of in bins labeled as "biohazards".

Sharps Disposal

- Do not recap needles (this makes it clear that they are used instead of new).
- Leave needles on syringes to prevent injury from trying to remove them.
- To prevent aerosolization of remaining solutions, do not clip needles.
- Discard used needles along with whatever they are attached it; do not try to detach the needle.

Medication Safety

The two organizations that work to understand the causes of medication errors are The Joint Commission (TJC) and the Institute for Safe Medication Practices (ISMP). A medication error is any preventable event that can lead to medication misuse or patient harm. A pharmacy technician should know their company's policies and procedures for reporting medication errors. The ISMP also has a confidential and voluntary program for reporting medication and vaccine errors; it uses these reports to learn about causes of errors.

Common causes of medication errors include: look-alike and sound-alike medication names, use of error prone abbreviations, drug name suffixes, and OTC brand name extensions.

Look-alike/Sound-alike Medications

Look-alike/Sound-alike medications are drugs that look alike or sound alike, but are very different drugs.

Below is a list of common look-alike/sound-alike drugs. See https://www.ismp.org/Tools/confuseddrugnames.pdf for a complete list of confused drug names.

Drug	Confused With
Adderall	Inderal
Apidra	Spiriva
Benadryl	benazepril
Bidex	Videx
Celexa	Zyprexa
Depakote	Depakote ER
Desyrel	Seroquel
Enjuvia	Januvia
Flonase	Flovent
folic acid	folinic acid
Granulex	Regranex
Hespan	heparin
iodine	Lodine

Kapidex	Casodex
levothyroxine	liothyronine
methadone	ketorolac
Mucinex	Mucomyst
Oxycontin	oxycodone
Paxil	Taxol, Doxil, Plavix
Restoril	Risperdal

Drug Name Suffix Confusion

Some drugs are available in various time-release formulations with different dosing frequencies. Manufacturers add "suffixes" or "modifiers" (e.g., Depakote ER or Cardizem CD) to medication names to indicate that the formulation is different from the immediate-release version. Since there is no standardization of drug suffixes, different suffixes can be used for an identical formulation by two different manufacturers or even similar suffixes for different formulations. A patient may get the wrong dosing if, for example, Wellbutrin XL is dispensed instead of Wellbutrin SR.

OTC Brand Name Extension Confusion

Brand name extension is when a company uses a well known proprietary name to introduce a new drug that may contain a different active ingredient. For example, Maalox contains aluminum–magnesium hydroxide and simethicone, but Maalox Total Stomach Relief contains bismuth subsalicylate. A pharmacy technician should help patients select the right drug with the correct active ingredients.

Error Prevention Strategies For Data Entry

Below is a list of strategies to prevent errors during data entry.
- Verify patient identity. Use at least 2 patient identifiers (e.g., name, birth date, address, etc.). The date of birth should be written on every hard copy prescription so the pharmacist has a second identifier readily available during verification.
- Verify patient information matches the information on the prescription.
- Verify patient allergies, concomitant medications, contraindications, etc. Allergy and medical condition (e.g., pregnancy) information should be updated in the patient's profile at each patient encounter and communicated to the pharmacist.

- All alerts that involve medication interactions, allergies, duplications, and other clinical warnings should be relayed to the pharmacist.
- If any part of the prescription is unclear or missing, contact the prescriber to clarify the information.
- Verify with the patient that the treatment prescribed is appropriate/expected.
- Allow entry of only one patient's prescription at a time to void mix-ups.
- Always use "baskets" to keep a patient's prescriptions separate from others.

Patient Package Insert and Medication Guide Requirements

Prescription drugs must have a container label and product labeling. Product labeling is also known as "package insert" or "prescribing information". The "package insert" should contain the following information: clinical pharmacology, indications and usage, contraindications, warnings, precautions, adverse reactions, drug abuse and dependence, dosage, and packaging.

Patient Package Inserts (PPI) are required by the FDA for potentially dangerous drugs; it must include a table of contents and a summary of the risks and benefits of the drug. PPIs are required for oral contraceptives and products containing estrogen. The PPI should provide information on how to safely use the product and must be provided to the patient with the first dispensing and with refills if 30 days has passed since the patient received a PPI.

Manufacturers may voluntarily provide Medication Guides (MedGuides) for some drugs; it provides information on how to safely use the drug and avoid adverse events. FDA requires that Medication Guides be issued with certain prescribed drugs and biological products when the Agency determines that:

- certain information is necessary to prevent serious adverse effects
- patient decision-making should be informed by information about a known serious side effect with a product, or
- patient adherence to directions for the use of a product are essential to its effectiveness.

Poison Prevention Packaging Act

The Consumer Products Safety Commission was created to reduce the risks associated with manufactured products; they do not regulate drugs, but they to do regulate the containers that drugs are sold in. The Poison Prevention Packaging Act was created to prevent the death of young children; it requires the use of child-resistant caps.

There are some exceptions to the child-resistant packaging due to concerns about accessibility of medications to the elderly and handicapped. With the exception of prescription drugs, manufacturers of certain household products that are regulated under the PPPA have the option of marketing one size in a conventional package as long as that same product is supplied in a popular-sized package, which is child-resistant.

Some products that are exempted from the PPPA include the following:

- Powdered unflavored aspirin
- Effervescent aspirin
- Sublingual nitroglycerin
- Oral contraceptives
- Hormone replacement therapy
- Powdered iron preparations
- Effervescent acetaminophen
- Hydrocarbon-containing products where the liquid cannot flow freely

Issues That Require Pharmacist Intervention

Drug Utilization Review (DUR)

DUR is a review strategy performed by pharmacists to review a patient's prescriptions, health history, and medication data. DURs are conducted for every prescription to prevent adverse drug events (ADE) and check appropriateness of treatment. During the DUR, the pharmacist should check the following:
- Any type of drug interaction (drug-drug interaction, drug-disease interaction, etc.)
- Appropriateness of treatment
- Correct length of treatment
- Medication overuse/misuse/abuse
- Need for drug dosage modification
- Need for therapeutic substitutions

Adverse Drug Events (ADE)

An adverse drug event is an undesired side effect of a drug that can harm a patient. ADEs can be caused by various factors such as patient allergies, drug interactions, incorrect dosages, etc.

OTC Recommendations

Pharmacy technicians should never counsel patients; only pharmacists can counsel patients and provide recommendations. Technicians can take patient medical history, including both prescription and OTC drugs the patient is taking, and provide that information to the pharmacist.

Therapeutic Substitutions

Pharmacists may recommend therapeutic substitutions (substitution of a drug with another therapeutically equivalent drug) based on various factors such as cost, patient allergies, drug interactions, etc.

Drug Misuse/Abuse

Drug misuse is medication taken for any reason other than for which it was prescribed; it can be intentional or unintentional.

Missed Dose

Pharmacists should inform patients on what to do if they miss a dose as most patients assume that they can just take the missed dose with the next dose, which is not always the case.

High Alert Medications

High alert medications are medications you need to pay special attention to because they can cause significant harm when calculation or other errors are made. Always have another person double check the calculations.

Classes of High Alert Medications:
- adrenergic agonists, IV (e.g., EPINEPHrine, phenylephrine, norepinephrine)
- adrenergic antagonists, IV (e.g., propranolol, metoprolol, labetalol)
- anesthetic agents, general, inhaled and IV (e.g., propofol, ketamine)
- antiarrhythmics, IV (e.g., lidocaine, amiodarone)
- antithrombotic agents, including:
  - anticoagulants (e.g., warfarin, low molecular weight heparin, IV unfractionated heparin)
  - Factor Xa inhibitors (e.g., fondaparinux, apixaban, rivaroxaban)
  - direct thrombin inhibitors (e.g., argatroban, bivalirudin, dabigatran etexilate)
  - thrombolytics (e.g.,alteplase, reteplase, tenecteplase)
  - glycoprotein IIb/IIIa inhibitors (e.g.,eptifibatide)
- cardioplegic solutions
- chemotherapeutic agents, parenteral and oral
- dextrose, hypertonic, 20% or greater
- dialysis solutions, peritoneal and hemodialysis
- epidural or intrathecal medications
- hypoglycemics, oral
- inotropic medications, IV (e.g., digoxin, milrinone)
- insulin, subcutaneous and IV
- liposomal forms of drugs (e.g., liposomal amphotericin B) and conventional counterparts (e.g., amphotericin B desoxycholate)
- moderate sedation agents, IV (e.g., dexmedetomidine, midazolam)
- moderate sedation agents, oral, for children (e.g., chloral hydrate)

- narcotics/opioids
    - IV
    - transdermal
    - oral (including liquid concentrates, immediate and sustained-release formulations)
- neuromuscular blocking agents (e.g., succinylcholine, rocuronium, vecuronium)
- parenteral nutrition preparations
- radiocontrast agents, IV
- sterile water for injection, inhalation, and irrigation (excluding pour bottles) in containers of 100 mL or more
- sodium chloride for injection, hypertonic, greater than 0.9% concentration

Specific High Alert Medications:
- EPINEPHrine, subcutaneous
- Epoprostenol (Flolan), IV
- Insulin U-500
- Magnesium sulfate injection
- Methotrexate, oral, non-oncologic use
- Opium tincture
- Oxytocin, IV
- Nitroprusside sodium for injection
- Potassium chloride for injection concentrate
- Potassium phosphates injection
- Promethazine, IV
- Vasopressin, IV or intraosseous

Source: https://www.ismp.org

Common Safety Strategies

The most important step of identifying drugs is using the correct drug name. All drug information is based upon communicating the correct drug name.

Do Not Use Error Prone Abbreviations

Every accredited health-care system is required to have a "Do Not Use" list of dangerous abbreviations, acronyms, and symbols that will not be used. In addition to that, TJC also has a "Do Not Use" list which is shown below:

Do Not Use	Potential Problem	Use Instead
U (for unit)	Mistaken as zero, four, or cc.	Write "unit"
IU (for international unit)	Mistaken as IV (intravenous) or 10 (ten)	Write "international unit"

Q.D., QD, q.d., qd (daily); Q.O.D., QOD, q.o.d, qod(every other day)	Mistaken for each other. Period after the Q mistaken for "I" and the "O" mistaken for "I".	Write "daily" Write "every other day"
Trailing zero (X.0 mg) Lack of leading zero (.X mg)	Decimal point is missed	Never write a zero by itself after a decimal point (X mg), and always use a zero before a decimal point (0.X mg)
MS MSO4 and MgSO4	Can mean morphine sulfate or magnesium sulfate. Confused for one another.	Write "morphine sulfate" Write "magnesium sulfate"

Tall Man Lettering

Tall man letters are capital letters used to emphasize different parts of drug names to help distinguish between look-alike/sound-alike names. See examples below.

Drug Name With Tall Man Letters	Confused With
acetaZOLAMIDE	acetoHEXAMIDE
buPROPion	busPIRone
DOBUTamine	DOPamine

Leading and Trailing Zeroes

Leading Zeroes
You should avoid "naked" decimal points. For example, .5 mg can easily be confused for 5 mg; you should write 0.5 mg instead.

Trailing Zeroes
You should avoid trailing zeroes for whole numbers. For example, 5.0 mg can easily be confused for 50 mg; you should write 5 mg instead.

Separating Inventory

- Look alike/sound alike medications should be placed on separate shelves.
- High alert medications should be stored away from regular medications.
- Medications with similar formulations should be grouped together so that you only need to look at a specific area for the formulation needed.

NCCMERP Recommendations

The National Coordinating Council For Medication Error Reporting and Prevention (NCCMERP) recommends the following to prevent medication errors (Source: The Pharmacy Technician, pg. 38-39):

1. Prescriptions should always be reviewed by a pharmacist before dispensing. Any concerns should be addressed using an established process.
2. Patient profiles should be current and complete.
3. Dispensing areas should be designed to reduce fatigue (e.g., adequate lighting, noise level abatement, air conditioning, etc.); minimize distractions (e.g., less clutter and personal interruptions); and sufficient staffing should be provided.
4. Products should be arranged so that it is easy to distinguish medications from one another (e.g., use of signs or markers).
5. Medication should be double checked for accuracy before dispensing; either by another individual or automated computer system.
6. Labels should be read at least 3 times: when selecting the drug, when packaging the drug, and when returning the drug to the shelf.
7. The pharmacy staff should triple check filling of medication stock or automated dispensing machines/cabinets for accuracy. This should be done when selecting the drug, before the drug leaves the pharmacy, and before putting the drug in the automated dispensing machine/cabinet.
8. Pharmacists should counsel the patient on the following: indications of use; precautions and warnings; potential adverse reactions; interactions with other food or medications; what to do in case of adverse reactions; and storage requirements.
9. Pharmacies should collect and analyze data regarding actual and potential medication errors for quality improvement.
10. Pharmacies should establish procedures for medication dispensing and provide initial and ongoing training to staff.

Pharmacy Quality Assurance

A quality assurance program is a system of standard operating procedures (SOPs) and reviews to assure the quality, safety, and efficacy of the care or treatment delivered. Reviews/audits are done to ensure that standard operating procedures were followed. Quality assurance programs should also have a way to detect and track errors and develop ways to correct deficiencies.

Quality Assurance Practices For Inventory Control

Many pharmacies have computerized inventory control systems. Monitoring inventory is important to ensure that the pharmacy has an adequate supply of drugs and awareness of drugs that may be expiring soon. Accurate data entry is critical and the use of barcodes can reduce data entry errors.

The inventory system should keep track of the National Drug Code (NDC) number of a medication. The NDC number uniquely identifies a drug (including strength and dosage form) and is used to identify a drug during safety recalls.

Risk Management Guidelines And Regulations

Use the following guidelines to manage risk and prevent errors:
- Patient information (including allergies, medical history, medications) should be checked every time.
- Include fail-safes or forcing functions in the process; for example, the cash register could be integrated with a computer system that prevents an order from completing unless a pharmacist has verified the order.
- Use automation and computerization such as barcode scanning, robots to count pills, e-prescribing to avoid human errors.
- Use standardization when possible to reduce complexity (i.e. used standardized prescription forms, etc.)
- Use redundancies, reminders, and checklists. For example, use independent double checks for high alert medications, counsel patients about medications, etc.

Source: Kaborsi-Tadros, pg. 150

A quality related event (QRE) is any error in the dispensing or administration of a drug. The State Board of Pharmacy requires that QREs be documented and maintained on the day of the incident. The document must include a description of the event and the actions taken. Root cause analysis (RCA) is the process of examining what factors may have led to an error occurring.

Communication

Communication between pharmacists, pharmacy technicians, patients, and all those involved in completing a prescription order is vital. Information regarding product recalls and shortages must be communicated between the FDA, manufacturers, pharmacists, and patients. Pharmacy technicians and pharmacists often have to communicate with other doctors, nurses, insurance personnel regarding prescription refills, prior authorizations, and other prescription filling issues. Pharmacists must counsel patients on the proper and safe usage of the prescribed drugs.

Pharmacists and technicians should be trained on how to deal with customer complaints. When handling patient complaints, use the acronym HEAT: Hear the patient, Empathize with the patient, Apologize, and Take action.

Medication Order Entry and Fill Process

A medication order in a hospital environment is equivalent to a prescription in a retail pharmacy.

Prescriptions must contain the following information:
- Patient's name and address
- Prescriber's name, title, office address, phone number
- Prescriber's DEA number (required on all controlled substance prescriptions)
- Prescriber's National Provider Identifier (NPI)
- Date prescription was written. Non-controlled prescriptions are typically good for a year; controlled prescription laws vary by state.
- Signa (directions for use)
- Drug name and strength
- Drug quantity
- Refill instructions
- Dispense as written (DAW) code or signature line indicating that a brand or generic drug is being dispensed.
- Signature of prescriber

Order Entry and Fill Process

Retail

1. The technician receives a prescription. Prescriptions can be brought in by the patient or patient's representative. Prescribers can also send prescriptions electronically, by fax, or telephone.
2. The technician gathers patient info (name, date of birth, allergies, current medications, medical history, etc.), insurance info, prescriber name and enters the data into the computer system. If this is a refill, it will have the same prescription number as the original prescription.
3. The computer processes the information and alerts the technician if there are any potential drug safety or payment concerns that require a DUR. **Pharmacists must check all DUR messages.**
4. After the prescription and billing information is adjudicated (whether the insurance company rejects or accepts the claim), the computer prints out labels and receipts. The receipt contains copayment information.
5. The technician prepares the medication.
   a. Retrieves medication from the stock shelf and scans the stock bottle barcode against the label barcode to verify that the correct drug was retrieved.
   b. Check the expiration date on the drug.

c. Measure the correct amount of drugs and put it in the correct container. Child proof containers are required by law unless the patient requests easy-open caps. If the patient requests non child resistant caps, document that information in the patient's records.

d. Place label on the container.

e. The pharmacist performs a final verification that the prescription is filled accurately. Depending on state laws, either the pharmacist or technician affixes any auxiliary labels and provides patient package inserts and medication guides.

6. The patient receives the medication, signs the pharmacy's notice of HIPAA compliance if they've never signed one before, and the technician rings the sale.

7. The pharmacists provide patient counseling. The pharmacist should provide counseling for all new prescriptions, DUR alerts, and per pharmacy protocol on refills. A signature log is used to document that the customer picked up the prescription and received or denied counseling from the pharmacist.

Hospital

In a hospital, the central pharmacy is where drugs are compounded, prepared, and separated into unit doses. Everyday, a list of medications that need to be prepared, for a 24 hour period, is determined and the pharmacy technician is then responsible for preparing and labelling the needed medications. After the pharmacist verifies the orders, the pharmacy technician delivers the orders to the nursing units and puts the medications into the automated dispensing machine. Pharmacy technicians are also responsible for ensuring adequate inventory levels for the automated dispensing machines. When a technician delivers medications, they should also keep a census of the number of patients still in the hospital and the number of patients discharged; for discharged patients, the technician will return unused medications back to the central pharmacy and destroy unused IV medications.

Nurses record medication orders on a medication administration record (MAR). The MAR contains a record of all medication ordered for a patient, time medication was delivered, and who administered the medication over a 24 hours period.

There are several types of medication orders. **Standing orders or scheduled medication orders** are for drugs that are given at scheduled intervals throughout the day. Pharmacy technicians will prepare enough of a scheduled order to last 24 hours. **PRN orders** are for medications on an as needed basis. **STAT orders** are for medications needed right away. **Controlled substance medication orders** are for orders that contain narcotics that require documentation of dispensing and administration. All medications given to patients are unit-dosed.

1. A prescription is written on a medication order form or entered into a computerized physician order entry (CPOE) system. Patient information is gathered by other healthcare professionals and includes the following information:

     a. Patient name, birthdate, and identification number (medical record number)

     b. Patient room number

     c. Height, Weight, and Laboratory Values (all of which may be needed to calculate dosage)

     d. Diagnosis, if available

2. A pharmacist receives and reviews the prescription.
3. A pharmacist or technician enters the order.
4. A pharmacy technician prepares the medication. Depending on hospital protocol, either another pharmacist or technician checks the order.
5. The medication is transported by robot, technician, or pneumatic tube to a patient's nursing unit.
6. The nurse administers the medication and records it in the MAR.

Pharmacy Abbreviations/Prescription Interpretation

The prescription Signa or Sig is written with common abbreviations. The Signa provides the prescription instructions. Below is a list of common abbreviations you should know. Source: The Pharmacy Technician, pg. 206.

Routes of Administration

Abbreviation	Meaning
ad	Right ear
as, al	Left ear
au	Each ear
od	Right eye
os, ol	Left eye
ou	Each eye
po	By mouth
SL	sublingually
top	topically
pr	rectally
pv	vaginally
inh	inhalation
per neb	By nebulizer

SC, subc, subq	subcutaneous
im	intramuscular
iv	intravenous
ivp	Intravenous push
ivpb	Intravenous piggyback

Dosage Form

Abbreviation	Meaning
tab	tablet
cap	capsule
SR, XR, XL	slow/extended release
sol	solution
susp	suspension
syr	syrup
liq	liquid
supp	suppository
crm	cream
ung, oint	ointment

Frequency

Abbreviation	Meaning
bid	Twice a day
tid	Three times a day
qid	Four times a day
am/q am	morning/each morning
pm	Afternoon or evening
hs	At bedtime
prn	As needed

ac	Before food/meals
pc	After food/meals
stat	immediately
q	every
qh	Every hour
q2h	Every 2 hours

Units of Measure

Abbreviation	Meanings
i, ii, etc.	One, two, etc.
ss	One half
gtt	drop
mL	milliliter
tsp	Teaspoon (5 mL)
tbsp	Tablespoon (15 mL)
fl oz	Fluid ounce (30 mL)
L	liter
mcg	microgram
mg	milligram
G, g, gm	gram
mEq	milliequivalent
aa	Of each
ad	Up to
aq ad	Add water up to
qs, qs ad	Add sufficient quantity to make

Other

Abbreviation	Meaning

UD	As directed
NR	No refill
DAW	Dispense as written
w	with
w/o	without

Calculate Doses Required

Pharmacy technicians will often have to calculate days supply. Days supply is the number of days the prescribed quantity of drugs will last when taken as directed. It is important that days supply is calculated correctly for insurance reimbursement purposes and for preventing interruption of therapy. Insurance companies will typically only allow a refill once 75% of the previous fill has been reached, so submitting an incorrect days supply could cause an insurance company to deny a refill that should have been allowed.

For examples of how to calculate days supply, see section Days Supply under Pharmacy Math.

Labeling Requirements

Manufacturer Stock Label

The manufacturer stock label contains information such as : National Drug Code (NDC) number, NATO Stock Number (NSN), lot number, expiration date, active ingredients and their strength, storage requirements, type of dispensing container required, DEA order form requirement, manufacturer's name and address, drug form, brand and generic name, legend statement, and package quantity. The NDC number is a manufacturer assigned identification number for the drug. It consists of 3 sets of number: the first set of numbers tells you who the manufacturer is; the second set tells you the medication, strength, and dosage; the third set of numbers tells you the package size. The NSN is the identification number is recognized in all NATO countries and identifies material items of supply.

Prescription Label

Many states have different prescription label requirements, but the minimum set of requirements are: name and address of dispenser, prescription serial number, date filled, name of prescriber, name of patient, expiration date, number of refills, directions for use, and cautionary statements. Directions for use should begin with a verb (take, apply, inhale, etc.), indicate route of administration, and use whole words (not abbreviations). The FDA requests, but does not require, that the label include the National Drug Code (NDC) number. The NDC is a unique 10 digit number that identifies the drug and is used to confirm that the correct drug was selected.

Auxiliary Labels

Auxiliary labels provide specific warnings such as Take With Food, May Cause Drowsiness, Shake Well, Keep Refrigerated, etc. Auxiliary labels are affixed onto the container.

Unit Dose Labels

Unit dose labels are placed on unit dose packages. Unit dose packages contain a single dose of medication and is often used in institutional or hospital pharmacies. Unit dose labels should contain the name, strength, manufacturer, lot number, expiration date, and dosage form.

Packaging Requirements

All prescriptions must be dispensed with child-resistant caps unless specifically requested otherwise.

Since the chemical composition of a drug may be altered by exposure to light, drugs should be dispensed in containers that have adequate light resistance.

Some drugs, such as nitroglycerin, can bind with the PVC in containers which may affect the efficacy of the drug. In these situations, you should use a glass container because glass is inert/non-reactive.

Automated Dispensing Systems

Retail

Many retail pharmacies have automated counting systems such as Parata Max. The system contains unique barcoded cells that hold different drugs. To reduce errors, a technician scans the barcode on the stock bottle and the system cell to ensure drugs are loaded into the correct cell. When the system receives a prescription, it will count, fill, cap, and label the prescription.

Hospital

Many hospitals have automated dispensing cabinets (ADC) such as Pyxis Med/Supply Station, Omnicell, etc.. ADCs are located throughout a hospital and allows healthcare providers to gain access to drugs. The systems keeps a record of which drugs/supplies were taken by which nurse and for which patient.

Unit-dose medication re-packing systems are used create unit doses from pharmacy stock.

IV and TPN compounding devices can automatically compound sterile ingredients into a single IV bag without manual intervention from a technician.

Centralized narcotic dispensing and tracking devices help keep track of controlled substances.

Pharmacy Inventory Management

Inventory management is a large part of the pharmacy technician's job. To maintain an adequate supply of drugs, pharmacies use a perpetual inventory system that maintains a continuous record of all items in inventory so that you can always see what stock is available. A perpetual inventory system is a requirement for Schedule II substances. Perpetual inventory of Schedule II drugs must be handwritten and signed by a pharmacist when the Schedule II drug is received, dispensed, or disposed; it must also be reconciled every 10 days.

It is important to only purchase from well known or established wholesalers. The Drug Supply Chain Security Act (DSCSA) requires the use of an electronic tracking system so that pharmacies know where a medication was manufactured and shipped.

Formulary

A formulary is a list of medications approved for use in the pharmacy. An open formulary is one that allows the purchase of any medication that is prescribed. A close formulary is a limited list of approved medications. In some hospitals, a drug on the formulary that is therapeutically equivalent may be substituted for a drug not on the formulary. The formulary is continually updated as new information about drug side effects/contraindication is available, resulting in drugs being added or removed from the formulary.

NDC, Lot Numbers, And Expiration Dates

The National Drug Code (NDC) is a 10 digit 3 segment number. The first segment identifies the labeler or manufacturer. The second segment identifies the package strength, dosage form, and formulation. The third segment identifies the package form and size. The NDC is used to verify that the correct drug was retrieved when filling a prescription.

The lot number is usually stamped on the side of the drug packaging. The lot number is a unique number issued by a manufacturer. It is important to know the lot number because the lot number is used to identify the affected drugs during a recall.

Expiration dates are usually set to 1 year from the date the medication is packaged or manufacturer's expiration date, whichever comes first. If the expiration date doesn't specify the day of month a drug expires, it is assumed to expire on the last day of the month. Medications that are reconstituted, such as IV medications, also have a beyond use date. Depending on distributor/manufacturer policies, expired drugs may be returned for reimbursement.

Ordering And Receiving Processes

Pharmacies use Periodic Automatic Replenishment (PAR) systems to maintain an adequate supply of drugs based on reorder points. Reorder points are minimum and maximum inventory levels for a drug. When the minimum reorder point is reached, the system will automatically purchase enough of the drug to reach the maximum inventory level for that drug. Turnover rate is the number of days it takes to use the complete stock of an item; this is important to know for quality and spoilage issues. Rotate stock by placing new products behind old products; this will help with dispensing drugs before they expire.

When receiving an order:
- Use barcodes to identify an item
- Every item in shipments, invoices, and purchase orders must be reconciled
- Verify the strength and amount of each item is correct
- Check for broken or damaged stock

For checks and balances, the person ordering the drug should not be receiving the drug; this is especially important for controlled substances.

Storage Requirements

Store drugs with look-alike names on different shelves to help prevent errors. Store newer items behind older ones to make sure older medication is dispensed first.

Drugs should be stored according to manufacturer instructions. Most drugs should be kept at a temperature of 68F to 77F.

Drugs that need to be refrigerated should be stored at temperatures between 36F to 46F. Refrigerators should be plugged into an outlet marked for emergency use so in case of a power outage, it will switch to use emergency power generators. If refrigerated medication is left out too long, they should be discarded. Refrigerator temperatures should be checked twice a day.

Drugs that are to be kept in a "Dry Place" should be stored in a place where humidity does not exceed 40%.

Removal

Medications that have expired or cannot be completely used before the expiration date must be discarded or returned to the manufacturer. Expired investigational drugs should be returned to the study sponsor. Besides expiration, drugs that are damaged or recalled can also be returned to the manufacturer. The information usually required for returning a product includes original purchase order number, item number, quantity, and reason for return.

Reverse Distributors

Reverse distributors specialize in returning expired and discontinued products to manufacturers. They are responsible for filling out all paperwork necessary (including paperwork for Class II drugs and controlled substances) for reimbursement. They charge pharmacies a percentage of the return credit for their services.

Disposal

Due to the federal Safe Water Drinking Act, pharmacies must follow OSHA, EPA, and DOT regulations for the safe disposal of drugs. There are companies that specialize in the safe disposal of medications.

Pharmacy Billing and Reimbursement

Customers pay for medication using private insurance plans, public insurance plans, or cash. Most insurance plans require customers to meet a deductible; a deductible, or co-insurance, is the amount the patient must pay in a benefit period before the insurance will pay a portion of the cost of the prescription. The copay is the portion of the medication price that a patient must pay. Some insurance have dual copays; this means that there is a lower copay for generic drugs and a higher copay for brand name drugs with no generic equivalent.

Reimbursement Policies And Plans

Private Insurance Plans

Patients with prescription drug coverage are issued prescription drug benefit cards with billing and co-pay information on them.

Health Maintenance Organizations (HMOs)

HMOs are a network of providers that work for or contract with an HMO. HMOs usually only cover medications that are in-network and often require generic substitutions.

Preferred Provider Organizations (PPOs)

PPOs are a network of providers that contract with the insurer, but will partially reimburse patients for services incurred outside of the PPO network. PPOs often also require generic substitutions.

Public/Government Insurance Plans

Medicare

Medicare is a federal program administered by the Centers for Medicare and Medicaid Services (CMS). Medicare covers those over 65 years old, disabled people under 65, and those with kidney failure or ALS.
- Medicare Part A covers hospital services, including care from a nursing facility and hospice care.
- Medicare Part B, for an additional premium, covers outpatient services, doctor visits, medical supplies, and preventive services.
- Medicare Part C (Medicare Advantage Plan) is a health plan offered by private insurers to provide Part A and Part B benefits.
- Medicare Part D (Medicare Prescription Drug Plan), for an additional premium, covers prescription drugs. Participants are subject to deductibles and copays.

Medicaid

Medicaid is a federal-state program that provides medical coverage for individuals or families with low incomes; it may also cover those with disabilities. The individual states decide who is eligible and what will be covered. Each state's Medicaid program has its own formulary; drugs not on the formulary may not be covered and prior authorization form must be submitted and accepted to dispense a non-formulary drug. Some states require patients to pay a small copay and some states require a Share-of-Cost; in Share-of-Cost, patients are required to meet a monthly payment before Medicaid will start to cover for medical expenses.

VHA and TRICARE

The Veterans Health Administration (VHA) provides benefits to veterans. It generally only covers prescriptions written by VA doctors and filled at VA pharmacies.

TRICARE provides benefits to eligible uniformed service members, retirees, and family members. There are 3 types of coverage:
- Standard: a fee-for-service cost-sharing plan
- Extra: a PPO plan
- Prime: an HMO plan with a Point of Service (POS) plan

Pharmacy benefits are administered through a Pharmacy Benefit Manager (PBM) which has access to a network of military pharmacies.

Other Plans

Worker's Compensation Plans

Worker's compensation plans provide benefits to those injured on the job. Claims are billed directly to the patient's worker's compensation plan.

Patient Assistance Programs

Pharmaceutical manufacturers have patient assistance programs to help patients that don't have insurance and need medication they cannot afford. Patients and their physician must fill out and submit an application to the manufacturer.

Pharmacy Benefit Managers

Many HMOs, PPOs, etc. use pharmacy benefit managers (PMB) or third party administrators (TPA) to collect payments from patients; PMBs and TPAs are essentially the middlemen between insurance companies and patients.

Third Party Resolution/Reimbursement

Online Claim Information Required

The following information is usually needed for online claim processing.

Cardholder/member identification number	DAW code
Group number (identifies employer or other group insurance plan)	Quantity dispensed
Name of patient	Days supply
Sex	Prescriber's ID number
Birth date	Pharmacy National Provider Identifier
Relationship to cardholder	Ingredient cost
Date prescription is written	Dispensing fee
Date prescription is dispensed	Total price
Is this a new prescription or refill	Deductible and copay amount
National Drug Code	Balance due
Pharmacy Benefit International Identification Number (BIN). The BIN identifies the third party payer.	

DAW Dispensing Code:

0 = no product selection indicated	5 = brand name dispensed at generic price
1 = substitution not allowed by provider	6 = override
2 = substitute allowed, patient requested brand	7 = substitution not allowed, brand name required by law
3 = substitute allowed, pharmacist selected brand	8 = substitute allowed, brand name drug not available
4 = substitute allowed, generic drug not in stock	9 = other

Once a technicians gathers the necessary information from the patient and enters it into the computer, billing information is transmitted online to the insurer or PBM. Within minutes, the technician should receive a response indicating whether the claim was approved or rejected, drug/disease interaction alerts, benefit amount, and copay information.

If a generic drug is available and dispensed, it is reimbursed with the maximum allowable cost (MAC). If only a brand name drug is available, reimbursement is based on the average sale price (ASP) or the wholesale acquisition cost (WAC).

For Medicaid reimbursements, the average manufacturer's price (AMP) is used to determine the federal upper limits (FUL) payment.

Insurers or PBMs require hard copies of every prescription and hard copies or electronic signature logs for all claims submitted electronically.

Rejected Claims

Pharmacy technicians can call the insurance plan's help desk to help determine coverage and resolve issues with rejected claims. Some common reasons for rejected claims include:
- Not having prior authorization. Each insurance company has its own prior authorization list. Drugs on that list require physician to get approval from the insurance company before prescribing the drug. This process may take 24-48 hours. If a prior authorization is not granted, the patient can still receive the drug, but will have to pay 100% of the cost.
- Dependent exceeds plan's age limit
- Birth date, person code, or sex does not match the information in the insurer's record
- Prescriber is not a network provider. Medicaid and HMOs often require prescribers to be in their network.
- Patient is refilling too soon or refills must be done through a mail order pharmacy.
- Drug is not in the insurer's formulary and will be rejected; sometimes insurers will approve a drug not in the formulary if there is a prior authorization granted.
- Plan limit or days supply exceeded. A lesser amount should be dispensed and number of refills adjusted.

Healthcare Reimbursement Systems

Reimbursement in settings such as home health, long-term care, and home infusion is usually handled as a fee-for-service or episode-of-care system. In a fee-for-service system, the provider is paid a fee for each service they provide. In an episode-of-care system, providers are paid for the condition they treat.

Coordination Of Benefits

Sometimes families will have two different insurance plans; this requires a coordination of benefits to maximize coverage, but not exceed 100% of cost. For example, one plan can be billed for the prescription and the other plan can be billed for the copay.

When coordinating benefits, you must determine which plan should provide primary coverage and which plan should provide secondary coverage and submit the claim in that order. Patients with both public and private insurance must submit claims to the private insurance before the public insurance.

Pharmacy Information System Usage and Application

Most pharmacies use Pharmacy Information Systems (PIS) to manage patient, prescription, and inventory data. PIS consists of a collection of interconnected pharmacy software and databases. Databases are where information or data is stored and should be backed up nightly. Electronic medical records are stored in databases. To protect patient privacy, access to all data needs to be secured at all stages (collection of data, transmission of data, and storage of data) and social security information should not be stored in pharmacy databases.

The National Council for Prescription Drug Program (NCPDP) is responsible for establishing standards for the electronic transmission/exchange of information. In particular, SCRIPT is a standard set by the NCPDP for transferring prescription, medical history, and insurance information.

PIS can also help generate reports such as:

Diversion report: A report about theft or loss of controlled substances.
Inventory report: A report on pharmacy inventory.
Override report: A report used to tell you about pharmacy personnel users that "override" or disregard warnings or safety measures.
Usage report: A report that tells you about the pattern of usage for a particular medicine.

Practice Test 1

1. Calculate the days supply for the following prescription:
   Synthroid 75 mcg, i cap po bid, dispense 90
   a. 15 days
   b. 30 days
   c. 45 days
   d. none of the above

2. Methadone is a Schedule ___ drug?
   a. I
   b. II
   c. III
   d. IV

3. ___ is a standard set by the NCPDP for e-prescribing.
   a. SCRIPT
   b. VAERS
   c. PIS
   d. PMB

4. How should a laminar flow hood be cleaned?
   a. bottom to top, back to front away from the HEPA filter
   b. bottom to top, front to back towards the HEPA filter
   c. top to bottom, front to back towards the HEPA filter
   d. top to bottom, back to front away from the HEPA filter

5. All of the following are examples of computer input devices, except:
   a. Mouse
   b. Keyboard
   c. Microphone
   d. Computer monitor

6. Drugs ending with ___ are considered antipsychotics.
   a. -perone
   b. -pidem
   c. -peridone
   d. -oxetine

7. A doctor writes a prescription for Synthroid with DAW code of 1, can levothyroxine be dispensed instead?
   a. Yes
   b. No

8. Which technique should be used to mix two powders into a homogenous mixture?
   a. geometric dilution
   b. Trituration
   c. Levigation
   d. none of the above

9. How often should pharmacy databases be backed up?
    a. Nightly
    b. Weekly
    c. Bi-weekly
    d. Monthly

10. Synthroid costs $50 for 90 capsules. What will it cost the patient to buy 30 capsules if the pharmacy adds a 25% markup and $15.00 dispensing fee?
    a. $16.66
    b. $20.82
    c. $35.82
    d. $45.82

11. Which identification number is assigned to health care providers to transmit health information?
    a. Member identification number
    b. Medical group identification number
    c. NPI
    d. BIN

12. Which of the following is incorrect?
    a. 0.5 mL
    b. 5.0 mL
    c. 5.5 mL
    d. 5.05 mL

13. What type of water should be used for sterile preparations? Select all that apply.
    a. water for injection USP
    b. sterile water for injection USP
    c. purified water USP
    d. bacteriostatic water for injection USP

14. Which plan provides coverage for individuals or families with low income?
    a. Medicare
    b. Medicaid
    c. Worker's Compensation
    d. Patient Assistance Programs

15. Erythrocin is a type of ?
    a. Antibiotic
    b. Antihistamine
    c. Antiviral
    d. Antifungal

16. The amount a patient must pay in a benefit period before insurance will pay a portion is called ?
    a. the deductible
    b. the premium
    c. the copay
    d. dual copay

17. Lumigan is used to treat which condition?
    a. Ulcers
    b. Glaucoma
    c. Conjuntivitis
    d. High blood pressure
18. Drugs that must be stored in a "Dry Place" should not be exposed to humidity exceeding
    a. 20%
    b. 40%
    c. 60%
    d. 80%
19. Which form must be filled out before destroying a controlled substance?
    a. DEA 41
    b. DEA 106
    c. DEA 222
    d. None of the above
20. When taking inventory, which of the substances must be counted exactly? Select all that apply.
    a. schedule II
    b. schedule III
    c. schedule IV substances in containers that hold more than 1000 tablets/capsules
    d. schedule V
21. How many grams of dextrose is there in a 100 mL IV bag containing a 25% dextrose solution?
    a. Not enough information
    b. 25 grams
    c. 50 grams
    d. None of the above
22. How often should refrigerator temperatures be checked?
    a. once a day
    b. twice a day
    c. every 4 hours
    d. every 6 hours
23. All but which of the following information is required by an insurance company when processing a claim?
    a. DAW code
    b. drug expiration date
    c. patient name
    d. patient sex
24. For all claims submitted electronically, insurers require _____. Select all that apply.
    a. hard copies of the prescription
    b. hard copies or electronic signature logs
    c. hard copies of the receipt

25. A perpetual inventory system is required for which of the following substances? Select all that apply.
    a. Schedule II
    b. Schedule III
    c. Schedule IV
    d. Schedule V
26. What is a turnover rate?
    a. the amount of a drug sold in a year
    b. how often stock is rotated
    c. how often a drug is returned to a manufacturer due to expiration
    d. the number of days it takes to use the complete stock of an item
27. How often can Schedule III or IV prescriptions be refilled?
    a. They may be refilled as specified by the prescriber.
    b. They may be refilled up to 3 times within 6 months after the issue date.
    c. They may be refilled up to 5 times within 6 months after the issue date.
    d. They may never be refilled.
28. Which set of numbers in the NDC number should you look at to determine the medication strength?
    a. First set
    b. Second set
    c. Third set
    d. Fourth set
29. The suffix "-megaly" means?
    a. Enlargement
    b. Weakness
    c. Softening
    d. Tumor
30. When is a prescriber's DEA number required to be included on a prescription?
    a. it is never required
    b. when prescribing controlled substances
    c. only when prescribing chemotherapy agents
    d. only when prescribing injectable medications
31. What is the prefix for "double"?
    a. Dia
    b. Dipl
    c. Dis
    d. Dys
32. How do you write the number 24 in roman numeral?
    a. XXVI
    b. XXV
    c. XXIV
    d. None of the above
33. The drug repackaging log must include the following information. Select all that apply.

a. Pharmacist's initials

b. Technician's initials

c. Lot number

d. Prescriber's name

34. Which of the following is not required on an inpatient medication label?

a. Drug lot number

b. Location of the patient

c. Expiration date

d. None of the above

35. Incomplete DEA 222 forms must be kept for 2 years.

a. True

b. False

36. What is the abbreviation for "slow/extended release"? Select all that apply.

a. SR

b. ER

c. XR

d. XL

37. What is the abbreviation for "as needed"?

a. asn

b. an

c. prn

d. pn

38. What does the root word "cutane" mean?

a. Skull

b. Brain

c. Skin

d. none of the above

39. How many times can a prescription be refilled if the prescriber did not specify the number of refills allowed?

a. 0

b. 1 time if not a Schedule II drug

c. 2

d. 3

40. A "May Cause Drowsiness" auxiliary label should be placed on which of the following medications?

a. Antihistamines

b. Oral corticosteroids

c. ADHD medications

d. Antispasmodic drugs

41. What does the following sig mean?

ii gtt ou tid

a. two drops in each ear, two times a day

      b. two drops in each ear, three times a day

      c. two drops in left ear, two times a day

      d. two drops in each eye, three times a day

42. A prescriber indicates that a generic substitution is allowed, however the generic drug is not in stock. What DAW code should be used?

      a. 1

      b. 2

      c. 3

      d. 4

43. A patient has a prescription that reads

    Sig: 1-2 drops au daily

    How should this medication be used?

      a. left ear

      b. right ear

      c. each ear

      d. each eye

44. A patient has a prescription that reads

    Sig: 1 tab pc tid

    How should this medication be used?

      a. twice a day

      b. after meals

      c. at night

45. The abbreviation for "by mouth" is

      a. po

      b. bm

      c. pr

      d. im

46. After putting on gloves, you should spray with gloves with 70% isopropyl alcohol.

      a. True

      b. False

47. Patients with both public and private insurance must:

      a. choose one plan to submit the claim to

      b. submit claim to the public insurance before the private insurance

      c. submit claim to the private insurance before the public insurance

      d. submit claim to both the public and private insurance simultaneously

48. Drugs that need to be refrigerated should be stored at what temperature?

      a. 68F to 78F

      b. 36F to 46F

      c. 46F to 56F

      d. 56F to 66F

49. When disposing sharps, separate the syringe from the needle and cover the needle to prevent accidental injury to others.

      a. True

b.   False

50. According to NCCMERP recommendations, labels should be read when ____. Select all that apply.
    a.   selecting the drug
    b.   packaging the drug
    c.   returning the drug to the shelf

51. You can find a complete list of drug recalls on which organizations website?
    a.   FDA
    b.   USP
    c.   TJC
    d.   ISMP

52. Which organization sets the standards for the identity, strength, quality, and purity of medications, dietary supplements, and food ingredients?
    a.   FDA
    b.   USP
    c.   TJC
    d.   ISMP

53. A quality related event (QRE) is
    a.   any incident where the patient is unhappy with the services provided
    b.   any error in the dispensing or administration of a drug
    c.   any issue involving the quality or efficacy of a drug

54. Restoril and Risperdal are examples of:
    a.   drug name suffix confusion
    b.   otc brand name extension confusion
    c.   look-alike/sound-alike medication
    d.   tall man lettering

55. Epinephrine, Oxytocin, Vasopressin and Insulin U-500 are all examples of
    a.   narcotics
    b.   drugs that require IV administration
    c.   high alert medications
    d.   schedule I drugs

56. Instead of writing QD, you should write
    a.   daily
    b.   every other day
    c.   by mouth
    d.   by ear

57. A patient prescriptions is refilled every 60 days. Is a Patient Package Insert required every time the prescription is filled?
    a.   Yes
    b.   No

58. Which of the following is on the "Do Not Use" list of abbreviations? Select all that apply.
    a.   U
    b.   IU

c. MS

d. None of the above

59. A pharmacy technician is allowed to answer which of the following questions? Select all that apply.

    a. What are the side effects of a drug?

    b. What is the dosage form?

    c. What are other recommended brands of the drug?

    d. What is the route of administration?

60. Which of the following statements regarding leading and trailing zeroes is true?

    a. Always include a trailing zero. Always include a leading zero.

    b. Always include a trailing zero. Never include a leading zero.

    c. Never include a trailing zero. Always include a leading zero.

    d. Never include a trailing zero. Never include a leading zero.

61. Which of the following are considered high alert medications?

    a. Narcotics

    b. parenteral nutrition preparations

    c. sterile water for injection

    d. none of the above

62. What are examples of instabilities when compounding solutions? Select all that apply.

    a. Miscibility

    b. precipitate formation

    c. Discoloration

    d. uncharacteristic odor

63. All work should be done at least ___ inside a laminar workstation to prevent contamination.

    a. 2 inches

    b. 4 inches

    c. 6 inches

    d. 8 inches

64. Desyrel and Seroquel are considered look-alike/sound-alike drugs.

    a. True

    b. False

65. VHA provides coverage at _____. Select all that apply.

    a. any public pharmacy

    b. any public hospital

    c. any retail pharmacy

    d. any VA pharmacy

66. You need to compound a slow release ointment, which ointment base should you use?

    a. Water miscible base

    b. Aqueous base

    c. Oil base

    d. None of the above

67. Compounded oral preparations containing water should have beyond use dates:

a. No later than 14 days stored at a controlled cold temperature

b. No later than 30 days

c. The earliest expiration date of any ingredient or 6 months, whichever is earlier

d. None of the above

68. Chemotherapy agent should be compounded inside a sterile environment such as a laminar airflow workstation.

a. True

b. False

69. A drug recall in which the product has a strong likelihood of causing serious adverse effects is class ____ recall.

a. I

b. II

c. III

d. IV

70. A patient is taking 6 mL twice a day of amoxicillin 200 mg/3 mL. How many mg of amoxicillin is the patient taking?

a. 12 mg

b. 400 mg

c. 600 mg

d. 800 mg

71. What should the pharmacy technician do if the patient does not want child resistant caps?

a. Refuse to fill the order

b. Request authorization from the pharmacist

c. Have the patient fill a release of liability form

d. Document the request in the patient's record

72. The Combat Methamphetamine Epidemic Act requires all OTC drugs that contain ____ to be kept behind the pharmacy counter. Select all that apply.

a. Ketamine

b. Propoxyphene

c. ephedrine

d. pseudoephedrine

73. Which of the following is part of the restricted drug program? Select all that apply.

a. Isotretinoin

b. Thalidomide

c. Ketamine

d. Clozapine

74. If the pharmacies involve do not share an online database, how often can Schedule III, IV, and V original prescriptions be transferred?

a. 0

b. 1

c. 2

d. As often as the maximum number of refills allowed on the original prescription.

75. Drug suffixes are standardized.
   a. True
   b. False

76. A prescription for morphine may be faxed if the patient lives in a long term care facility.
   a. True
   b. False

77. What form must be filled to destroy a controlled substance?
   a. DEA 41
   b. DEA 106
   c. DEA 222
   d. None of the above

78. Which class of drugs can be kept openly on storage shelves. Select all that apply.
   a. Schedule I
   b. Schedule II
   c. Schedule III
   d. Schedule IV
   e. Schedule V

79. Antibiotics can reduce the effectiveness of which of the following?
   a. Claritin (antihistamine)
   b. Xalatan (anti-glaucoma)
   c. Prozac (antidepressant)
   d. Yav

80. Which of the following does not need to be shaken before use ?
   a. Emulsions
   b. Suspensions
   c. Elixirs

81. What did the Omnibus Budget Reconciliation Act (OBRA) require?
   a. patient privacy
   b. data backups
   c. pharmacists to provide patient counseling
   d. reporting of unlabelled/unexpected adverse reactions

82. Which of the following works by preventing calcium from entering cells of the heart and blood vessel walls?
   a. Brocrinat
   b. Diltiazem
   c. Fostedil
   d. Desmopressin

83. Sumatriptan is used to treat which condition?
   a. Depression
   b. Migraines
   c. Ulcers
   d. High cholesterol

84. How many tablespoons are in 45 mL?
   a. 3 tablespoons
   b. 5 tablespoons
   c. 9 tablespoons
   d. 15 tablespoons

85. What is a common side effect of ACE inhibitors? Choose all that apply.
   a. Increased blood pressure
   b. Coughing
   c. Low potassium levels
   d. Increased angiotensin II

86. Lansoprazole is indicated for the treatment of
   a. Ulcers
   b. Anxiety
   c. Depression
   d. High blood pressure

87. A drug with the suffix "-aril" belongs to which class of medications?
   a. Diuretics
   b. Beta-blockers
   c. Antivirals
   d. antifungals

88. What should be avoided when taking warfarin? Select all that apply.
   a. Antibiotics
   b. Aspirin
   c. Leafy Greens
   d. None of the above

89. A patient is covered under Medicare Part A and B; what services are covered? Select all that apply.
   a. hospital services
   b. doctor visits
   c. medical supplies
   d. prescription drugs

90. Epinephrine, Oxytocin, Vasopressin and Insulin U-500 are all examples of
   a. Narcotics
   b. drugs that require IV administration
   c. high alert medications
   d. Schedule I drugs

Practice Test 1 Answers

1. C. (1 day / 2 capsules) * (90 capsules) = 45 days supply

2. B. Methadone is a Schedule II drug. Some states require Schedule II drugs to be stored in locked narcotics cabinets.

3. A. SCRIPT is a standard set by the NCPDP for e-prescribing.

4. D. Laminar flow hoods should be cleaned top to bottom, back to front away from the HEPA filter.

5. D. A computer monitor is a computer output device.

6. C. Drugs ending with -peridone are antipsychotics. Drugs ending with -perone are anti-anxiety agents. Drugs ending with -pidem are hypnotics/sedatives. Drugs ending with -oxetine are antidepressants.

7. B. A Dispense As Written (DAW) code of 1 means substitution is not allowed.

8. A. Geometric dilution is a technique used to mix two powders of unequal quantity into a homogenous mixture. Trituration is the process of grinding powders to reduce particle size. Levigation is a technique used to reduce particle size by triturating it with a liquid.

9. A. Pharmacy databases should be backed up nightly.

10. C.
    ($50 /90 capsules) * 30 capsules = $16.66 for 30 capsules
    $16.66 + (16.66 * 0.25) = $20.82
    $20.82 + $15 (markup) = $35.82

11. C. The National Provider Identifier is assigned to health care providers to transmit health information.

12. B. 5.0 mL is incorrect. Never write a zero by itself after a decimal point (X mg), and always use a zero before a decimal point (0.X mg).

13. A,B,D. Only water for injection USP, sterile water for injection USP, or bacteriostatic water for injection USP should be used for sterile compounding.

14. B. Medicaid is a federal-state program that provides medical coverage for individuals or families with low incomes; it may also cover those with disabilities.

15. A. Erythrocin is a type of antibiotic.

16. A. The deductible is the amount a patient must pay in a benefit period before insurance will pay a portion.

17. B. Lumigan is a brand name for brimatoprost, which is used to treat glaucoma.

18. B. Drugs that must be stored in a "Dry Place" should not be exposed to humidity exceeding 40%.

19. A. To destroy controlled substances, you must use a DEA 41 form. The DEA 222 form, a triplicate form, is used to receive, order, or return Schedule II controlled substances. If a controlled substance is lost or stolen, the pharmacy must notify the nearest DEA diversion office and the local police department. It must also fill out a DEA 106 form.

20. A,C. Schedule II drugs must be counted exactly, but Schedule III, IV, and V drugs can be estimated. The exception to the estimated count would be for containers that hold more than 1,000 tablets or capsules. In that case, an exact count of the contents of the container must be undertaken.

21. B. 25 grams. Concentrations are expressed as weight to volume (g/100mL) or volume to volume (mL/100mL) or weight to weight (g/100g).

22. B. Refrigerator temperatures should be checked twice a day.

23. B. The drug expiration date is not required by an insurance company when processing a claim.

24. A,B. Insurers or PBMs require hard copies of every prescription and hard copies or electronic signature logs for all claims submitted electronically.

25. A. To maintain an adequate supply of drugs, pharmacies use a perpetual inventory system that maintains a continuous record of all items in inventory so that you can always see what stock is available. A perpetual inventory system is a requirement for Schedule II substances. Perpetual inventory of Schedule II drugs must be handwritten and signed by a pharmacist when the Schedule II drug is received, dispensed, or disposed; it must also be reconciled every 10 days.

26. D. Turnover rate is the number of days it takes to use the complete stock of an item; this is important to know for quality and spoilage issues.

27. C. Schedule III or IV prescriptions may be refilled up to 5 times within 6 months after the issue date. Schedule III or IV prescriptions can be partially filled any amount of time so long as the total quantity dispensed matches the total quantity prescribed within the 6 months.

28. B. The NDC number is a manufacturer assigned identification number for the drug. It consists of 3 sets of number: the first set of numbers tells you who the manufacturer is; the second set tells you the medication, strength, and dosage; the third set of numbers tells you the package size.

29. A. The suffix "-megaly" means enlargement.

30. B. A prescriber's DEA number is required when prescribing controlled substances.

31. B. Dipl means double; dia means completely; dis means separate; dys means painful or difficult.
32. C. XXIV = 24.

33. A,B,C,D. The repackaging log must include the following information: repackaging date, drug's name, drug's strength, dosage form, manufacturer's name, lot number, manufacturer's expiration date, beyond use date, repackaged quantity, technician's initials, pharmacist initials, prescriber's name.

34. D. Lot number, expiration date, location of patient are all required for an inpatient medication label.

35. A. All DEA 222 forms, even those that are incomplete or illegible, must be kept for 2 years.

36. A,C,D. The abbreviation for "slow/extended release" can be SR,XR, or XL.

37. C. "prn" is the abbreviation for "as needed".

38. C. "cutane" means skin.

39. A. Prescriptions cannot be refilled if the prescriber did not specify the number of refills allowed.

40. A,D. Antihistamines and antispasmodic drugs often cause drowsiness.

41. D. two drops in each eye, three times a day

42. D. DAW Code 4 (substitute allowed, generic drug not in stock). 1 = substitution not allowed by provider. 2 = substitute allowed, patient requested brand. 3 = substitute allowed, pharmacist selected brand.

43. C. au is an abbreviation for each eye.

44. A

45. A. The abbreviation for "by mouth" is po

46. A. After washing your hands, you should put on sterile gloves. Spray hands with sterile 70% isopropyl alcohol and allow to dry. Put on sterile gloves; gloves should cover the sleeves of the gown. Spray both gloves with 70% isopropyl alcohol

47. C. If a patient has both public and private insurance, a claim must be submitted to the private insurance before the public one.

48. B. Most drugs should be stored at 68F to 78F, but refrigerated drugs should be stored at 36F to 46F.

49. B. Leave needles on syringes to prevent injury from trying to remove them. Do not recap needles (this makes it clear that they are used instead of new).

50. A,B,C. Labels should be read at least 3 times: when selecting the drug, when packaging the drug, and when returning the drug to the shelf.

51. A. You can find a complete of drug recalls on the FDA's website.

52. B. The United States Pharmacopeia sets the standards for the identity, strength, quality, and purity of medications, dietary supplements, and food ingredients. The FDA enforces the USP standards.

53. B. A quality related event is any error in the dispensing or administration of a drug.

54. C. Look-alike/Sound-alike medications are drugs that look alike or sound alike, but are very different drugs.

55. C. They are all examples of high alert medications. High alert medications are medications you need to pay special attention to because they can cause significant harm when calculation or other errors are made. Always have another person double check the calculations.

56. A. QD is on the list of "Do Not Use" abbreviations. Write "daily" instead.

57. A. Yes. A PPI must be provided to the patient with the first dispensing and with refills if 30 days has passed since the patient received a PPI.

58. A,B,C. "U" may be mistaken as zero, four, or cc; write "Unit" instead. "IU" may be mistaken for IV or 10; write "International Unit" instead. MS can mean morphine sulfate or magnesium sulfate.

59. B,D. Pharmacy technicians can not counsel a patient on the side effects of a drug or provide recommendations; only pharmacists can counsel patients and provide recommendations.

60. C. Never include a trailing zero. Always include a leading zero.

61. A,B,C. Narcotics, parenteral nutrition preparations, and sterile water for injection are all considered high alert medications.

62. B,C,D. Precipitate formation, discoloration, and uncharacteristics odors are signs of instability when compounding solutions.

63. C. All work should be done at least 6 inches inside the workstation since laminar flow air near the edge of a workstation may be contaminated.

64. A. True. Desryel and Seroquel are considered look-alike/sound-alike drugs.

65. D. The Veterans Health Administration (VHA) provides benefits to veterans. It generally only covers prescriptions written by VA doctors and filled at VA pharmacies.

66. C. Water miscible or aqueous bases release drugs quickly. Oil based ointment bases generally release drugs slowly and unpredictably.

67. A. Compounded oral preparations containing water should have beyond use dates no later than 14 days stored at a controlled cold temperature.

68. B. While chemotherapy agents require sterile compounding processes, do not use laminar airflow workstations to prepare chemotherapy agents or other hazardous drugs because laminar airflow workstations do not protect personnel nor the environment from hazards.

69. A. There are 3 recall classifications: Class I, Class II, Class III. Class I: There is a strong likelihood that the product will cause serious adverse effects or death. Class II: Product may cause temporarily but reversible adverse effects or there is little likelihood of serious adverse effects. Class III: Product is not likely to cause adverse effects.

70. D. (6 mL/ 1 dose) * (2 doses/ 1 day) * (200 mg/3 mL) = 800 mg/day

71. D. If a patient requests non-child resistant caps, fill the order and document the request in the patient's records.

72. C,D. All OTC drugs that contain ephedrine and pseudoephedrine must be kept behind the pharmacy counter.

73. A,B,D. Isotretinoin, Thalidomide, and Clozapine are part of the restricted drug program and have prescription processing requirements.

74. B. If the pharmacies do NOT share an online database, Schedule III, IV, and V original prescriptions may be transferred one time between the pharmacies. If the pharmacies share an online database, then Schedule III, IV, and V prescriptions may be transferred the same number of times as the maximum number of refills on the original prescription.

75. B. False. Since there is no standardization of drug suffixes, different suffixes can be used for an identical formulation by two different manufacturers or even similar suffixes for different formulations.

76. A. Morphine is a Schedule II drug. Schedule II prescriptions must be presented in person at the pharmacy except when a patient lives in a long term care facility, is in hospice care, or receives compounded home infusion or IV pain therapy. In those cases, a prescription with the prescriber's signature may be faxed.

77. A. A DEA 41 form must be filled out to destroy a controlled substance. A DEA 106 form must be filled out to report a loss or theft of a controlled substance. A DEA 222 form must be filled out to receive or order a controlled substance.

78. C,D,E. Schedule III, IV, and V drugs can be kept openly on storage shelves.

79. D. Antibiotics can reduce the effectiveness of contraceptives. Yav is a contraceptive. Claritin is an antihistamine. Xalatan is an anti-glaucoma drug. Prozac is an antidepressant.

80. C. Elixirs do not need to be shaken. Emulsions are a mixture of 2 liquids that are immiscible (cannot be mixed without the help of external forces such mixing, stirring, shaking, or addition of an emulsifier). In suspensions, active ingredients are mixed with a liquid, usually water, in which it cannot dissolve, so it must be shaken before use.

81. C. The OBRA act required that pharmacist provide patient counseling when dispensing a prescription.

82. B. Calcium channel blockers prevent calcium from entering cells of the heart and blood vessels, reducing blood pressure. Of the drugs listed, only diltiazem is a calcium channel blocker.

83. B. Migraine headaches are often treated with anti-inflammatory drugs such as aspirin, NSAIDS, and a class of drugs called "triptans".

84. A. 45 mL * (1 tablespoon/ 15 mL) = 3 tablespoons.

85. B. ACE inhibitors reduce blood pressure by preventing your body from producing angiotensin II (a substance that narrows your blood vessels and raises your blood pressure). ACE inhibitors may cause coughing and high levels of potassium; there are special warnings for usage during pregnancy. Common side effects include: dry cough, nausea, loss of appetite, upset stomach. Common drug interactions include: other blood pressure medications, insulin, diabetes medication, NSAIDS, arthritis medication, alcohol.

86. A. Lansoprazole is indicated for the treatment of ulcers.

87. C. Drugs with the suffix "-aril" belong to the antivirals class.

88. A,B,C. Warfarin has many serious drug interactions (especially with aspirin) and overdosing can cause life threatening conditions. Too much vitamin K in your diet can lower the effect of warfarin. Avoid eating large amounts of leafy green vegetables, as many of them contain large amounts of vitamin K. Many antibiotics decrease the effectiveness of birth control, cause photosensitivity, and have serious interactions with warfarin.

89. A,B,C. Medicare Part A covers hospital services, including care from a nursing facility and hospice care. Medicare Part B, for an additional premium, covers outpatient services, doctor visits, medical supplies, and preventive services. Medicare Part D (Medicare Prescription Drug Plan), for an additional premium, covers prescription drugs. Participants are subject to deductibles and copays.

90. C. They are all examples of high alert medications. High alert medications are medications you need to pay special attention to because they can cause significant harm when calculation or other errors are made. Always have another person double check the calculations.

Practice Test 2

1. Which of the following drugs should be avoided by those who have a sulfa allergy. Select all that apply.
    a. Sulfamethoxazole-trimethoprim
    b. Erythromycin-sulfisoxazole
    c. Septra
    d. Bactrim

2. If 50g of 1.5% retinol cream is mixed with 25g of 2.5% retinol cream, what is the concentration of drug in the final product?
    a. 1.5 %
    b. 1.8 %
    c. 2.0 %
    d. 2.2 %

3. Which of the following drugs should be kept on a separate shelf from hydromorphone?
    a. hydroxyzine
    b. hydralazine
    c. morphine
    d. none of the above

4. Which of the following is NOT needed when filing a claim?
    a. patient's name
    b. patient's sex
    c. patient's social security number
    d. national drug code

5. Schedule II prescriptions
    a. may not be refilled
    b. may be refilled up to 5 times within 6 months after the issue date
    c. may be refilled as specified by the prescriber

6. Calciferol is another name for which vitamin
    a. Vitamin B1
    b. Vitamin B5
    c. Vitamin C
    d. Vitamin D

7. A doctor orders DrugA 25mg/mL for a patient at 1 mL every 8 hours for 5 days. What is the total volume to be dispensed, in mL, if the only DrugA stock you have is 100mg/5mL?
    a. 15 mL
    b. 19 mL
    c. 25 mL
    d. 30 mL

8. Chemotherapy agent should be compounded inside a sterile environment such as a laminar airflow workstation.
    a. True
    b. False
9. How do you write the number 40 in roman numerals?
    a. IVX
    b. XXXX
    c. XL
    d. None of the above
10. If the expiration date is 05/2018, when does the drug expire?
    a. 05/01/2018
    b. 05/31/2018
    c. 04/30/2018
    d. 06/01/2018
11. Which of the following is an antiemetic? Select all that apply.
    a. Ceredase
    b. Imodium
    c. Phenergan
    d. Zofran
12. Which of the following is used to treat osteoporosis? Select all that apply.
    a. Adalimumab
    b. Alendronate
    c. Cyclobenzaprine
    d. risedronate
13. If the pharmacies share an online database, how often can schedule III, IV, or V drugs be transferred?
    a. Never
    b. one time
    c. same number of times as the maximum number of refills
    d. any number of time
14. Which of the following should be stored away from other medications? Select all that apply.
    a. Epinephrine
    b. Celexa
    c. Insulin U-500
    d. Zyprexa
15. If 10 grams of a compounded drug contains FakeDrugA and FakeDrugB in a 1:4 ratio, how many grams of FakeDrugA are there?
    a. 2 grams
    b. 2.5 grams
    c. 5 grams
    d. none of the above
16. A prescription reads:

Sig: 1 drop ad q2h

How should the medication be used?

    a. one drop in the left eye

    b. one drop in the right eye

    c. one drop in the left ear

    d. one drop in the right ear

17. Pharmacies can log and view transactions involving ephedrine and pseudoephedrine in

    a. MedWatch

    b. MethCheck

    c. TJC

    d. ISMP

18. The IV flow rate is 15 mL/hour. How long will a 120 mL IV bag last?

    a. 4 hours

    b. 8 hours

    c. 10 hours

    d. 12 hours

19. Any time you suspect a patient is taking drugs incorrectly, you should

    a. tell the patient that they are taking the drugs incorrectly and tell them the correct directions

    b. ask the patient to speak to the pharmacist for correct directions

    c. tell the patient to speak with their doctor

20. Patients with both public and private insurance must:

    a. choose one plan to submit the claim to

    b. submit claim to the public insurance before the private insurance

    c. submit claim to the private insurance before the public insurance

    d. submit claim to both the public and private insurance simultaneously

21. Which of the following drugs should be refrigerated? Select all that apply.

    a. Amoxil

    b. Benadryl

    c. Humira

    d. Tamiflu

22. How often is a complete inventory of controlled substances required?

    a. 1 year

    b. 2 years

    c. 3 years

    d. 5 years

23. Patients taking nitroglycerin should not also take _____. Select all that apply.

    a. sildenafil

    b. tadalafil

    c. vardenafil

    d. diflunisal

24. Which of the following is not required on a legal prescription?

    a. patient's name

b. patient's address

c. NDC number

d. Signa

25. Compounded oral preparations containing water should have beyond use dates:

    a. No later than 14 days stored at a controlled cold temperature

    b. No later than 30 days

    c. The earliest expiration date of any ingredient or 6 months, whichever is earlier

26. If the pharmacies share an online database, how often can schedule II drugs be transferred?

    a. Never

    b. one time

    c. same number of times as the maximum number of refills

    d. any number of time

27. A look-alike/sound-alike name for methadone is

    a. ketorolac

    b. metformin

    c. morphine

    d. none of the above

28. What should you reference when handling hazardous substances?

    a. The Book of Hazardous Substances

    b. Material Safety Data Sheets

    c. The Orange Book

    d. Drug Facts and Comparisons

29. What are reverse distributors?

    a. companies that pharmacies sell drugs to

    b. companies that manufacturers sell drugs to

    c. companies that specialize in returning expired products to manufacturers

    d. companies that deliver drugs to hospitals

30. When taking inventory, all Schedule II, III, IV, and V drugs must be counted and not estimated.

    a. True

    b. False

31. Which insurance plan covers those over 65 years old?

    a. Medicare

    b. Medicaid

    c. VHA

    d. TRICARE

32. How long must paper prescriptions be kept?

    a. 1 year

    b. 2 years

    c. 5 years

    d. forever

33. Is AB3245618 a valid DEA number?

a. Yes

b. No

34. There is risk of therapeutic duplication if _____ is taken when ibuprofen

    a. Naproxen

    b. Clindamycin

    c. Diazepam

    d. acyclovir

35. Which of the following must be on the label if a drug is repackaged? Select all that apply.

    a. manufacturer name

    b. lot number

    c. drug strength

    d. dosage form

36. Given a 15 mg/5 mL concentration of FakeDrugA. How many tablespoons are needed to obtain 90 mg of FakeDrugA?

    a. 1 tablespoon

    b. 2 tablespoons

    c. 3 tablespoons

    d. 4 tablespoons

37. What is a brand of bismuth subsalicylate?

    a. Aspirin

    b. Motrin

    c. Pepto Bismol

    d. Pepcid AC

38. When disposing needles, needles should be clipped to prevent solutions from leaking.

    a. True

    b. False

39. Which act required pharmacist to provide patient counseling before dispensing a prescription?

    a. OBRA

    b. VAERS

    c. HIPAA

    d. None of the above

40. A look-alike/sound-alike name for levothyroxine is

    a. liothyronine

    b. Synthroid

    c. iodine

    d. none of the above

41. How many mL of 5% amoxicillin should be mixed with 15% amoxicillin to get 30 mL of 7% amoxicillin?

    a. 6 mL

    b. 12 mL

    c. 18 mL

    d. 24 mL

42. Diuretics can cause low levels of potassium in the body. This is an example of:
    a. drug food interaction
    b. drug nutrient interaction
    c. drug dietary supplement interaction
    d. drug disease interaction

43. To uniquely identify patients, social security numbers should be stored in pharmacy databases.
    a. True
    b. False

44. A patient is prescribed two bottles of Tylenol 200 mg, 30 counts each, 2 capsule, 2 times a day. What is the days supply?
    a. 7
    b. 15
    c. 20
    d. 28

45. Schedule IV prescriptions
    a. may not be refilled
    b. may be refilled up to 5 times within 6 months after the issue date
    c. may be refilled as specified by the prescriber

46. Which Medicare program covers prescription drugs?
    a. Part A
    b. Part B
    c. Part C
    d. Part D

47. What is a generic substitute for Benadryl?
    a. paroxetine
    b. diphenhydramine
    c. metformin
    d. propranolol

48. Partial or emergency fills for Schedule II drugs may be dispensed if the pharmacist does not have enough supply to dispense the full amount; the remaining amount must be dispensed within
    a. 24 hours
    b. 48 hours
    c. 72 hours
    d. 80 hours

49. How many grams of dextrose are there in 250 mL of 35% dextrose solution?
    a. 35 g
    b. 70 g
    c. 88 g
    d. 98 g

50. If a pharmacy technician fails to observe a law, the supervising pharmacist is subject to a penalty by the state board.

a. True

b. False

51. What information must be recorded and maintained for recalled products? Select all that apply.

    a. date product was removed from inventory

    b. reason drug was removed

    c. dosage form of drug

    d. initials of technician and supervising pharmacist

52. A person earning minimum wage who was recently injured on the job is likely to be covered by

    a. Medicare

    b. Medicaid

    c. Worker's compensation

    d. TRICARE

53. Drug ABC has the following NDC number: 12345-1234-12. If the same manufacturer were to make another drug, what would a possible NDC number be?

    a. 12345-1111-11

    b. 11111-1234-11

    c. 11111-1111-12

    d. 11111-1111-11

54. Which of these is an example of therapeutic duplication?

    a. lansoprazole and omeprazole

    b. cyclobenzaprine and promethazine

    c. atenolol and albuterol

    d. amoxicillin and fluconazole

55. A patient comes in with a STAT prescription order while the pharmacist is out, you should

    a. dispense the medication since it's an emergency order

    b. ask the patient to wait for the pharmacist

    c. page for a pharmacist

56. Instead of writing "U", what should you write instead?

    a. Micro

    b. Milli

    c. Zero

    d. unit

57. After compounding a solution, you should check for signs of incompatibility. What is a visible sign of chemical incompatibility? Select all that apply.

    a. formation of gases

    b. formation of precipitate

    c. change in color

    d. uncharacteristic odor

58. To prevent errors in data entry, you must verify the patient's identity how at least how many patient identifiers?

    a. 1

    b. 2

    c. 3

    d. 4

59. Which of these drugs require a DEA 222 form?

    a. Methadone

    b. anabolic steroids

    c. Ketamine

    d. clonazepam

60. If a patient is prescribed 3 tbsp of amoxicillin a day. How many mL of amoxicillin will the patient take in a day?

    a. 15 mL

    b. 30 mL

    c. 45 mL

    d. 60 mL

61. Which of these is a brand of fluoxetine?

    a. Ativan

    b. Prozac

    c. Ambien

    d. Risperdal

62. Which of the following is an example of a drug disease interaction?

    a. beta blockers and asthma

    b. ginseng and heparin

    c. statins and grapefruit juice

    d. antihistamines and diazepam

63. Which auxiliary label should be placed on a bottle of clindamycin? Select all that apply.

    a. May Cause Drowsiness

    b. Keep Refrigerated

    c. Take With Food or Water

    d. Continue Medicine For Full Time of Treatment

64. A prescription reads:

Sig: i q6h prn pain

How often should the prescribed drug be taken?

    a. every 6 hours

    b. as needed for pain

    c. every 6 hours as needed for pain

    d. six times a day

65. HIPAA does NOT allow pharmacies to disclose PHI WITHOUT patient approval.

    a. True

    b. False

66. Disposable needles should always be used when preparing admixtures.

    a. True

    b. False

67. What reference should you consult when looking for a therapeutic equivalent for Synthroid?
    a. Safety Data Sheets
    b. The Orange Book
    c. Physician's Desk Reference
    d. None of the above

68. It costs $159.99 for 100 tablets of FakeDrugA. It is now on sale for 15% off. How much would 75 tablets cost?
    a. 75
    b. 102
    c. 123
    d. 132

69. Which of the following is on the "Do Not Use" list of abbreviations? Select all that apply.
    a. qd
    b. qod
    c. ad
    d. od

70. The theft of morphine must be reported to? Choose all that apply.
    a. FDA
    b. USP
    c. DEA
    d. Local police department

71. Which of the following class of drugs is considered high alert? Select all that apply.
    a. Antipsychotics
    b. Antiarrhythmics
    c. subcutaneous insulin
    d. hypoglycemics

72. What is a generic substitute for Zocor?
    a. Simvastatin
    b. Enalapril
    c. Nitroglycerin
    d. furosemide

73. A product is being recalled because there is a strong likelihood that it will cause serious adverse effects or death. What recall class is this?
    a. class I
    b. class II
    c. class III

74. Unit dose labels should contain which of the following fields? Select all that apply.
    a. drug name
    b. drug strength
    c. drug manufacturer
    d. drug dosage form

75. A prescription reads:

Sig: i po tid pc

When should the patient take the medication?

    a. twice a day, before meals

    b. twice a day, after meals

    c. three times a day, before meals

    d. three times a day, after meals

76. Recalls are listed in

    a. the manufacturer's report

    b. MedWatch

    c. FDA Enforcement Report

    d. ISMP

77. Pipettes are required for measuring volumes

    a. less than 1 mL

    b. less than 2 mL

    c. less than 5 mL

    d. less than 10 mL

78. A doctor has written a prescription with a DAW code of 1. What does this mean?

    a. substitute allowed, patient requested brand

    b. substitute allowed, pharmacist selected brand

    c. substitution not allowed by provider

    d. brand name dispensed at generic price

79. A brand name for tamsulosin is

    a. Flomax

    b. Fluzone

    c. Celexa

    d. Coumadin

80. A pharmacy sells $12,345 worth of drugs a month. The pharmacy makes a 15% profit. How much profit does the pharmacy make in a month?

    a. $1022

    b. $1852

    c. $2022

    d. $2852

81. The root word "adip" means?

    a. Hearing

    b. Fat

    c. Pain

    d. male

B. The root word "adip" means fat.

82. The abbreviation for right ear is?

    a. re

    b. ad

    c. as

d. al

B. The abbreviation for right ear is "ad". "as" and "al" mean left ear.

83. How long are Schedule II prescriptions valid for?
   a. 7 days
   b. 14 days
   c. 30 days
   d. 60 days

A. Schedule II prescriptions are valid for 7 days, after which, the prescriber must write a new prescription. Prescriptions can only be written for, at most, a 30 day supply and no refills.

84. The abbreviation "hs" means?
   a. before meals
   b. after meals
   c. every hour
   d. none of the above

D. The abbreviation "hs" means "at bedtime".

85. Emergency fills for a Schedule II prescription may not exceed a ___ day supply.
   a. 2
   b. 3
   c. 5
   d. 7

B. Emergency fills for a Schedule II prescription may not exceed a 3 day supply.

86. Which of the following medications require refrigeration? Select all that apply.
   a. amoxicillin
   b. insulin
   c. calcitonin
   d. latanoprost

A,B,C,D. All of the above medications require refrigeration.

87. Before a patient received their isotretinoin prescription, they must register with ?
   a. STEPS
   b. SCRIPT
   c. iPledge
   d. None of the above

C. Isotretinoin (Accutane) can cause serious adverse effects such as fetal abnormalities and death. Everyone who prescribes, dispenses, or uses isotretinoin (Accutane) must register with iPledge.

88. Risedronate is used to treat ?
   a. osteoporosis

     b. depression

     c. high blood pressure

     d. eczema

A. Risedronate is used to treat osteoporosis.

89. In what area should you perform activities such as opening boxes and garbing?
     a. DCA
     b. buffer area
     c. anteroom
     d. clean room

C. A clean room will contain a direct compounding area (DCA) where all compounding takes place. Next to the clean room is the buffer area. The buffer area is where components and supplies are gathered and prepared. The area directly outside the buffer area is called the anteroom. The anteroom is where personnel perform activities such as hand washing, garbing, label preparation, unpacking and opening or boxes, etc.

90. Clindamycin is used to treat ?
     a. Allergies
     b. Acne
     c. Eczema
     d. Cold

B. Clindamycin is used to treat acne.

Practice Test 2 Answers

1. A,B,C,D. Sulfamethoxazole-trimethoprim and erythromycin-sulfisoxazole both contain sulfonamides. Septra and Bactrim are sulfamethoxazole-trimethoprim brands.

2. B. First, figure out how many grams of retinol are are in each product and add them together to get the total grams of retinol:

$$\frac{50\,g}{1} \times \frac{1.5}{100} = 0.75\,g$$

$$\frac{25g}{1} \times \frac{2.5}{100} = 0.63\,g$$

0.75g + 0.63 g = 1.38 g of retinol total

Then, figure out how many grams of total product we have:
50g + 25g = 75g of total product

Then, divide total amount of retinol by the total amount of product and multiple by 100 to get the percentage:

$$\frac{1.38g}{75g} \times 100 = 1.8\%$$

3. C. Look-alike/sound-alike medications should be kept on separate shelves. Hydromorphone and morphine are look-alike/sound-alike medications.

4. C. The patient's social security number is not needed when filing a claim.

5. A. Schedule II prescriptions may not be refilled. Schedule III or IV prescriptions may be refilled up to 5 times within 6 months after the issue date. Schedule V and non-controlled drugs may be refilled as specified by the prescriber.

6. D. Calciferol is another name for Vitamin D.

7. B. First, figure out how many mL total is prescribed for 5 days.

$$\frac{1\,mL}{8\,hours} \times \frac{24\,hours}{1\,day} \times \frac{5\,days}{1} = 15\,mL$$

Then, figure out how many total mg of DrugA was prescribed.

$$\frac{25\,mg}{mL} \times \frac{15\,mL}{1} = 375\,mg$$

Then, figure out how many mL of the stock solution would give us 500 mg.

$$\frac{5mL}{100mg} \; \mathbf{X} \; \frac{375 \, mg}{1} = 18.75 \text{ mL}$$

8. B. While chemotherapy agents require sterile compounding processes, do not use laminar airflow workstations to prepare chemotherapy agents or other hazardous drugs because laminar airflow workstations do not protect personnel nor the environment from hazards.

9. C. XL is 40 in roman numerals. It cannot be XXXX beccause roman numerals cannot be repeated more than 3 times.

10. B. Expiration dates are usually set to 1 year from the date the medication is packaged or manufacturer's expiration date, whichever comes first. If the expiration date doesn't specify the day of month a drug expires, it is assumed to expire on the last day of the month. Medications that are reconstituted, such as IV medications, also have a beyond use date.

11. C,D. Phenergan (promethazine) and Zofran (ondansetron) are both antiemetics. Ceredase (alglucerase) is an enzyme. Imodium (loperamide) is an antidiarrheal.

12. B,D. Alendronate and risedronate are both used to treat osteoporosis. Adalimumab is an antirheumatic. Cyclobenzaprine is a muscle relaxant.

13. C. If the pharmacies do NOT share an online database, Schedule III, IV, and V original prescriptions may be transferred one time between the pharmacies. If the pharmacies share an online database, then Schedule III, IV, and V prescriptions may be transferred the same number of times as the maximum number of refills on the original prescription. Schedule II prescriptions cannot be transferred.

14. A,C. High alert medications should be stored away from other medications. Epinephrine and Insulin U-500 are high alert medications.

15. A. A 1:4 ratio means that for every 1 gram of FakeDrugA, there are 4 grams of FakeDrugB. There are a total of (1 + 4 = 5) parts. 1/5 is FakeDrugA and 4/5 is FakeDrugB. 10 grams x (1/5) = 2 grams.

16. D. "ad" means right ear.

17. B. The Combat Methamphetamine Epidemic Act (CMEA) requires all OTC drugs that contain ephedrine and pseudoephedrine to be kept behind the pharmacy counter. It also places a limit on the amount of ephedrine or pseudoephedrine that can be sold to an individual. Pharmacies can log and view transactions in MethCheck.

18. B. Using the formula and solve for X:

Flow rate = mL of IV solution / time

$$\frac{15\ mL}{hour} = \frac{120\ mL}{X}$$

X = 8 hours

19. B. Do not counsel patients, only pharmacists can counsel patients.
20. C. If a patient has both public and private insurance, a claim must be submitted to the private insurance before the public one.

21. A,C,D. Amoxil, Humira, and Tamiflu should be refrigerated.

22. B. A complete inventory of controlled substances is required every 2 years.

23. A,B,C. Patients taking nitroglycerin should not take sildenafil (Viagra), tadalafil (Cialis), or vardenafil (Levitra). Sildenafil, tadalafil, vardenafil may substantially increase the hypotensive effects of nitroglycerin. This is known as a drug-drug interaction.

24. C. NDC number is not required on a legal prescription. The following fields are required on a legal prescriptions: patient's name and address; prescriber's name, title, address, and number; prescriber's DEA number (required on all controlled substance prescriptions); prescriber's NPI; date; Signa; drug name, strength, quantity; refill instructions; DAW code; prescriber's signature.

25. A. Compounded oral preparations containing water should have beyond use dates no later than 14 days stored at a controlled cold temperature.

26. A. Schedule II prescriptions cannot be transferred. If the pharmacies do NOT share an online database, Schedule III, IV, and V original prescriptions may be transferred one time between the pharmacies. If the pharmacies share an online database, then Schedule III, IV, and V prescriptions may be transferred the same number of times as the maximum number of refills on the original prescription.

27. A. A look-alike/sound-alike name for methadone is ketorolac. See https://www.ismp.org/recommendations/confused-drug-names-list for a complete list of look-alike/sound-alike names.

28. B. You should reference the Material Safety Data Sheets when handling hazardous substances.

29. C. Reverse distributors specialize in returning expired and discontinued products to manufacturers. They are responsible for filling out all paperwork necessary (including

paperwork for Class II drugs and controlled substances) for reimbursement. They charge pharmacies a percentage of the return credit for their services.

30. B. Schedule II drugs must be counted, but Schedule III, IV, and V drugs can be estimated.

31. A. Medicare covers those over 65 years old, disabled people under 65, and those with kidney failure or ALS. Medicaid is a federal-state program that provides medical coverage for individuals or families with low incomes; it may also cover those with disabilities. The Veterans Health Administration (VHA) provides benefits to veterans. TRICARE provides benefits to eligible uniformed service members, retirees, and family members.

32. B. Paper prescriptions must be kept for 2 years. All electronic logs must be kept permanently.

33. B. No, it is not valid because the last digit should be 9.
To verify that the DEA number is valid, perform the following steps:
Add the 1st, 3rd, and 5th numbers (3 + 4 + 6 = 13); we'll call this SumOfGroup1.
Add the 2nd, 4th, and 6th numbers (2 + 5 + 1 = 8); we'll call this SumOfGroup2.
Multiply SumOfGroup2 by 2 (8 * 2 = 16); we'll call this Group2Doubled.
Add SumOfGroup1 and Group2Doubled (16 + 13 = 29); we'll call this the FinalValue.
The last digit in the FinalValue is called the "check digit" number and it should match the last digit in the DEA number.

34. A. Naproxen and ibuprofen are both NSAIDS.

35. A,B,C,D. Drugs that are repackaged must have the following on the label: generic drug name, drug strength, dosage form, manufacturer name and lot number, expiration date. It is extremely important to record the manufacturer name and lot number for recall and quality assurance purposes.

36. B. First, figure out how many mL are required to get 90 mg of the drug.

$$\frac{90 \, mg}{1} \times \frac{5 \, mL}{15 \, mg} = 30 \, mL$$

Given that 15 mL = 1 tablespoon, figure out how many tablespoons are in 30 mL.

$$\frac{30 \, mL}{1} \times \frac{1 \, tablespoon}{15 \, mL} = 2 \, tablespoons$$

37. C. Pepto Bismol is a brand of bismuth subsalicylate.

38. B. To prevent aerosolization of remaining solutions, do not clip needles.

39. A. The Omnibus Budget Reconciliation Act (OBRA) requires that pharmacist provide patient counseling. Vaccine Adverse Event Reporting System (VAERS) is a program maintained by the FDA to monitor vaccines. The Health Insurance Portability and Accountability Act (HIPAA) protects patient privacy and regulates the transfer of all patient health information electronically, on paper, or orally.

40. A. A look-alike/sound-alike name for levothyroxine is liothyronine. See https://www.ismp.org/recommendations/confused-drug-names-list for a complete list of look-alike/sound-alike names.

41. D. 24 mL of 5% amoxicillin is needed.

Higher % concentration		Desired % concentration minus lower % concentration. (let's call this box A)
	Desired % concentration	
Lower % concentration		Higher % concentration minus desired % concentration (let's call this box B)

Alligation Steps:
1. Fill in the boxes.
2. Add box A and box B to get the Total Parts.
3. To find the relative amount of the higher % concentration to use, divide Box A by the Total Parts.
4. To find the relative amount of the lower % concentration to use, divide Box B by the Total Parts.

15		(7 - 5) = 2
	7	
5		(15 -7) = 8

Total Parts : 2 + 8 = 10
Relative amount of higher % concentration to use: 2 / 10
Relative amount of lower % concentration to use: 8 / 10
mL of 15% amoxicillin needed = total mL desired * relative amount of higher %
$$= 30mL * (2/10) = 6 \text{ mL}$$
mL of 5% amoxicillin needed = total mL desired * relative mount of lower %
$$= 30mL * (8/10) = 24 \text{ mL}$$

42. B. Diuretics causing low levels of potassium in the body is an example of a drug nutrient interaction.

43. B. False. To protect patient privacy, social security numbers should not be stored.

44. B. First, figure out how many capsules are taken a day (2 capsules x 2 times a day = 4 capsules per day). Then, figure out how many total capsules there are in 2 bottles (2 bottles x 30 capsules per bottle = 60 capsules). Then, divide the total number of capsules by the number of capsules per day to get the days supply (60 capsules / 4 capsules per days) = 15.

45. B. Schedule II prescriptions may not be refilled. Schedule III or IV prescriptions may be refilled up to 5 times within 6 months after the issue date. Schedule V and non-controlled drugs may be refilled as specified by the prescriber.

46. D. Medicare Part D (Medicare Prescription Drug Plan), for an additional premium, covers prescription drugs. Medicare Part A covers hospital services, including care from a nursing facility and hospice care. Medicare Part B, for an additional premium, covers outpatient services, doctor visits, medical supplies, and preventive services. Medicare Part C (Medicare Advantage Plan) is a health plan offered by private insurers to provide Part A and Part B benefits.

47. B. Diphenhydramine is a generic substitute for Benadryl.

48. C. The remaining amount for Schedule II drug partial fills must be dispensed within 72 hours.

49. C. A 35% dextrose solution means that there are 35 grams of dextrose per 100 mL of solution. Set up the proportion as follows and solve for X:

$$\frac{35\ g}{100\ mL} = \frac{X}{250ml}$$

X = 87.5 g

50. A. True

51. A,B,C,D. The following information must be recorded and maintained for recalled products: date product was removed from inventory; name, strength, dosage form, and quantity of drug removed;manufacturer and lot number; reason drug was removed; initials of technician and supervising pharmacist.

52. C. Worker's compensation plans provide benefits to those injured on the job. Medicare covers those over 65 years old, disabled people under 65, and those with kidney failure or ALS. Medicaid is a federal-state program that provides medical coverage for individuals or families with low incomes; it may also cover those with disabilities. TRICARE provides benefits to eligible uniformed service members, retirees, and family members.

53. A. The NDC number is a manufacturer assigned identification number for the drug. It consists of 3 sets of number: the first set of numbers tells you who the manufacturer is; the second set tells you the medication, strength, and dosage; the third set of numbers tells you the package size.

54. A. Lansoprazole and omeprazole are both antiulcer drugs. Cyclobenzaprine is a muscle relaxant. Promethazine is an antiemetic. Atenolol is a beta-blocker. Albuterol is a bronchodilator. Amoxicillin is an antibiotic. Fluconazole is an antifungal.

55. C. Since it's a STAT (immediate) order, page for a pharmacist.

56. D. "U" is on the "Do Not Use" list of abbreviations. Write "unit" instead.

57. B,C. Signs of visible chemical instability of a solution include change in color or formation of a precipitate. Formation of gases or uncharacteristic odor are invisible signs of chemical instability.

58. B. Verify patient identity using at least 2 patient identifiers (e.g., name, birth date, address, etc.). The date of birth should be written on every hard copy prescription so the pharmacist has a second identifier readily available during verification.

59. A. The DEA 222 form is used to receive, order, or return Schedule II controlled substances. Methadone is a Schedule II controlled substance. Anabolic steroids and ketamine is a Schedule III drug. Clonazepam is a Schedule IV drug.

60. C. 1 tbsp = 15 mL so $\dfrac{3\ tbsp}{1} \times \dfrac{15\ mL}{1\ tbsp} = 45$ mL

61. B. Prozac is a brand of fluoxetine (an antidepressant). Ativan is a brand of lorazepam (anti-anxiety). Ambien is a brand of zolpidem (a sedative). Risperdal is a brand of risperidone (an antipsychotic).

62. A. Drug-disease interactions occur when a drug interacts or interferes with an existing medical condition. Beta-blockers taken for heart disease can worsen asthma. Ginseng and heparin is an example of a drug dietary supplement interaction. Dietary supplements

can interfere with the way a drug acts or how the body absorbs, uses, or disposes of the drug. Ginseng can increase the bleeding effects of heparin. Statins and grapefruit juice is an example of drug food interaction. Drug-food interactions occur when the effects of a drug are changed when taken with a particular food. Grapefruit juice should be avoided when taking statins because grapefruit juice decreases the metabolism of statins, causing a buildup of statins in the body which can lead to muscle and/or liver damage. Antihistamines and diazepam is an example of drug OTC interaction. OTC drugs can interact with prescription drugs. Antihistamines can cause drowsiness and intensify the sedative effects of prescription drugs such as diazepam, lorazepam, etc.

63. C,D. "Take With Food or Water" and "Continue Medicine For Full Time of Treatment" should be placed on a bottle of clindamycin.

64. C. The drug should be taken every 6 hours as needed for pain. q6h is an abbreviation for "every 6 hours". prn is an abbreviation for "as needed".

65. B. False. HIPAA does allow pharmacies to disclose PHI (the minimum necessary), WITHOUT patient approval, to others who are working on behalf of the patient such as physician offices and insurance/benefits management companies.

66. A. For sterility reasons, disposable needles should always be used when preparing admixtures.

67. B. Approved Drug Products with Therapeutic Equivalence and Evaluations (a.k.a - Orange Book). "Safety Data Sheets" provide information for handling hazardous substances. "Drug Facts and Comparisons" contains information on prescription and OTC drugs. "Physician's Desk Reference" is a compilation of medication package inserts and is updated every year.

68. B. First, figure out how much it would cost for 100 tablets at a 15% discount. Since there is a 15% discount, you will only be paying (100 - 15 = 85%) of the original price.
159.99 x 0.85 = 135.99
Then, figure out how much 1 tablet costs at the discounted price.
135.99 / 100 tablets = 1.36 per tablet
Then, figure out how much 75 tablets would cost at the discounted price.
1.36 x 75 = 102.

69. A,B. "qd" and "qod" are on the "Do Not Use" list; write "daily" and "every other day" instead. "ad" means "right ear". "od" means "right eye".

70. C,D. Morphine is a controlled substance. The theft of controlled substances must be reported to the DEA and local police department.

71. B,C,D. Antiarrhythmics, subcutaneous insulin, and hypoglycemics are all considered high alert medication.

72. A. Simvastatin, an antihyperlipidemic, is a generic substitute for Zocor. Enalapril is an ACE inhibitor. Nitroglycerin is an antianginal. Furosemide is a diuretic.

73. A. Class I: There is a strong likelihood that the product will cause serious adverse effects or death. Class II: Product may cause temporarily but reversible adverse effects or there is little likelihood of serious adverse effects. Class III: Product is not likely to cause adverse effects.

74. A,B,C,D. Unit dose labels should contain the name, strength, manufacturer, lot number, expiration date, and dosage form.

75. D. The patient should take 1 pill, by mouth, three times a day, after meals. "po" means by mouth. "tid" means 3 times a day. "pc" means after meals.

76. C. Recalls are listed in the weekly FDA Enforcement Report. MedWatch is a program maintained by the FDA that allows healthcare professionals to report adverse effects of a drug. The two organizations that work to understand the causes of medication errors are The Joint Commission (TJC) and the Institute for Safe Medication Practices (ISMP).

77. A. Pipettes are required for measuring volumes less than 1 mL.

78. C. A DAW code of 1 means substitution not allowed by provider.

79. A. A brand name for tamsulosin is Flomax. Tamsulosin is an alpha blocker.

80. B. The pharmacy makes $1852 in profits a month. 15% is equal to 15/100.
$$\frac{15}{100} \times 12{,}345 = 1851.75$$

81. B. The root word "adip" means fat.

82. B. The abbreviation for right ear is "ad". "as" and "al" mean left ear.

83. A. Schedule II prescriptions are valid for 7 days, after which, the prescriber must write a new prescription. Prescriptions can only be written for, at most, a 30 day supply and no refills.

84. D. The abbreviation "hs" means "at bedtime".

85. B. Emergency fills for a Schedule II prescription may not exceed a 3 day supply.

86. A,B,C,D. All of the above medications require refrigeration.

87. C. Isotretinoin (Accutane) can cause serious adverse effects such as fetal abnormalities and death. Everyone who prescribes, dispenses, or uses isotretinoin (Accutane) must register with iPledge.

88. A. Risedronate is used to treat osteoporosis.

89. C. A clean room will contain a direct compounding area (DCA) where all compounding takes place. Next to the clean room is the buffer area. The buffer area is where components and supplies are gathered and prepared. The area directly outside the buffer area is called the anteroom. The anteroom is where personnel perform activities such as hand washing, garbing, label preparation, unpacking and opening or boxes, etc.

90. B. Clindamycin is used to treat acne.

About the Exam

The Pharmacy Technician Certification Exam (PTCE) is a computer-based exam administered at Pearson VUE testing centers nationwide. It is a two-hour, multiple-choice, exam that contains 90 questions (80 scored questions and 10 unscored questions). You are not penalized for wrong answers so answer every question.

The PTCB uses a scaled scoring system with scores ranging from 1000 to 1600. 1400 is considered a passing score.

Below is a breakdown of the test content:

Knowledge Area	Percentage of exam
Pharmacology for Technicians	13.75%
Pharmacy Law and Regulations	12.5%
Sterile and Non-Sterile Compounding	8.75%
Medication Safety	12.5%
Pharmacy Quality Assurance	7.5%
Medication Order Entry and Fill Process	17.50%
Pharmacy Inventory Management	8.75%
Pharmacy Billing and Reimbursement	8.75%
Pharmacy Information Systems Usage and Application	10.00%

Thank You For Your Purchase

Thank you for your purchase. If you found this study guide helpful, please leave a review for us on Amazon; we would truly appreciate it.

If you have any questions or concerns, please contact us at goldstartestprep@gmail.com.

Appendix A: Top 200 Brand Name Drugs

Source: http://clincalc.com/DrugStats/Top200Drugs.aspx

Generic Name	Brand Name	Use
Lisinopril	Zestril	Antihypertensive
Levothyroxine	Synthroid	Hormone
Atorvastatin	Lipitor	Antihyperlipidemic
Metformin	Glucophage	Hormone
Simvastatin	Zocor	Antihyperlipidemic
Omeprazole	Prilosec	Antacid/Antiulcer
Amlodipine Besylate	Norvasc	Antihypertensive
Metoprolol	Lopressor	Antihypertensive
Acetaminophen; Hydrocodone Bitartrate	Vicodin	Opioid Analgesic
Albuterol	Ventolin	Bronchodilator
Hydrochlorothiazide	Microzide	Antihypertensive
Losartan Potassium	Cozaar	Antihypertensive
Gabapentin	Neurontin	Antiepileptic
Sertraline Hydrochloride	Zoloft	Antidepressant
Furosemide	Lasix	Antihypertensive
Acetaminophen	Tylenol	Analgesic
Atenolol	Tenormin	Antihypertensive
Pravastatin Sodium	Pravachol	Antihyperlipidemic
Amoxicillin	Amoxil	Antibiotic
Fluoxetine Hydrochloride	Prozac	Antidepressant
Citalopram	Celexa	Antidepressant
Trazodone Hydrochloride	Desyrel	Antidepressant
Alprazolam	Xanax	Sedative
Fluticasone	Flovent	Inhaled corticosteroid

Bupropion	Wellbutrin	Antidepressant
Carvedilol	Coreg	Antihypertensive
Potassium	Slow-K	Electrolyte
Tramadol Hydrochloride	Ultram	Analgesic
Pantoprazole Sodium	Protonix	Antacid/Antiulcer
Montelukast	Singulair	Immune modulator
Escitalopram Oxalate	Lexapro	Antidepressant
Prednisone	Sterapred	Hormone
Rosuvastatin Calcium	Crestor	Antihyperlipidemic
Ibuprofen	Motrin	Analgesic, NSAID
Meloxicam	Mobic	Analgesic,NSAID
Insulin Glargine	Lantus	Hormone
Hydrochlorothiazide; Lisinopril	Prinzide	Antihypertensive and diuretic combo
Clonazepam	Klonopin	Psychotropic
Aspirin	Bayer	NSAID and antiplatelet
Clopidogrel Bisulfate	Plavix	Anticoagulant
Glipizide	Glucotrol	Antidiabetic
Warfarin	Coumadin	Anticoagulant
Cyclobenzaprine	Flexeril	Muscle relaxant
Insulin Human	Humulin	Antidiabetic
Tamsulosin Hydrochloride	Flomax	Alpha blocker
Zolpidem Tartrate	Ambien	Sedative
Ethinyl Estradiol; Norgestimate	Ortho Tri-Cyclen	Contraceptive
Duloxetine	Cymbalta	Antidepressant
Ranitidine	Zantac	Antacid/Antiulcer
Venlafaxine Hydrochloride	Effexor	Antidepressant
Fluticasone Propionate; Salmeterol Xinafoate	Advair Diskus	Topical corticosteroid and bronchodilator combo
Oxycodone	Oxycontin	Opiate
Azithromycin	Zithromax	Antibiotic

Amphetamine	Adderall	Stimulant
Lorazepam	Ativan	Sedative
Allopurinol	Zyloprim	Antigout
Paroxetine	Paxil	Antidepressant
Methylphenidate	Ritalin	Psychotropic
Estradiol	Estring	Hormone
Hydrochlorothiazide; Losartan Potassium	Hyzaar	Antihypertensive
Ethinyl Estradiol; Norethindrone	Estrostep	Contraceptive
Fenofibrate	Tricor	Antihyperlipidemic
Propranolol Hydrochloride	Inderal	Antihypertensive
Glimepiride	Amaryl	Antidiabetic
Ergocalciferol	Calciferol	Vitamin
Esomeprazole	Nexium	Antacid/Antiulcer
Spironolactone	Aldactone	Antihypertensive
Loratadine	Claritin	Antihistamine
Naproxen	Aleve	NSAID
Lamotrigine	Lamictal	Antiepileptic
Hydrochlorothiazide; Triamterene	Dyazide	Antihypertensive
Cetirizine Hydrochloride	Zyrtec	Antihistamine
Sulfamethoxazole; Trimethoprim	Bactrim	Antibiotic
Lovastatin	Mevacor	Antihyperlipidemic
Diltiazem Hydrochloride	Cardizem	Antihypertensive
Clonidine	Catapres	Antihypertensive
Topiramate	Topamax	Antiepileptic
Amoxicillin; Clavulanate Potassium	Augmentin	Antibiotic
Pregabalin	Lyrica	Antiepileptic
Folic Acid	Folic Acid	Vitamin
Alendronate Sodium	Fosamax	Bisphosphonate
Hydrocodone Bitartrate	Zydone	Opiate

Amitriptyline	Elavil	Antidepressant
Diclofenac	Volteran	NSAID
Insulin Aspart	Novolog	Antidiabetic
Tiotropium	Spiriva	Bronchodilator
Quetiapine Fumarate	Seroquel	Antipsychotic
Enalapril Maleate	Vasotec	Antihypertensive
Bacitracin; Neomycin; Polymyxin B	Neosporin	Antibiotic
Sitagliptin Phosphate	Januvia	Antidiabetic
Diazepam	Valium	Sedative
Latanoprost	Xalatan	Antiglaucoma
Ciprofloxacin	Cipro	Antibiotic
Budesonide; Formoterol	Symbicort	Topical corticosteroid and bronchodilator combo
Hydroxyzine	Atarax	Antihistamine
Ethinyl Estradiol; Levonorgestrel	Alesse	Contraceptive
Docusate	Colace	Laxative
Valsartan	Diovan	Antihypertensive
Finasteride	Proscar	Urinary Retention
Ondansetron	Zofran	Anti-nausea
Ferrous Sulfate	Feosol	Hematopoietic
Cephalexin	Keflex	Antibiotic
Ezetimibe	Zetia	Antihyperlipidemic
Buspirone Hydrochloride	Buspar	Anti-anxiety
Donepezil Hydrochloride	Donepezil	Alzheimer
Lisdexamfetamine Dimesylate	Vyvanse	Stimulant
Insulin Detemir	Levemir	Antidiabetic
Tizanidine	Zanaflex	Muscle Relaxant
Celecoxib	Celebrex	NSAID
Amlodipine Besylate; Benazepril Hydrochloride	Lotrel	Antihypertensive

Doxycycline	Doryx	Antibiotic
Cyanocobalamin	Cyanocobalamin	Vitamin
Oxybutynin	Ditropan	Bladder relaxant
Isosorbide Mononitrate	Imdur	Nitrate
Morphine	Roxanol	Opioid
Insulin Lispro	Humalog	Antidiabetic
Hydralazine Hydrochloride	Apresoline	Antihypertensive
Levetiracetam	Keppra	Antiepileptic
Benazepril Hydrochloride	Lotensin	Antihypertensive
Divalproex Sodium	Depakote	Bipolar Disorder Treatment
Cholecalciferol; .Alpha.-Tocopherol	Cholecalciferol; .Alpha.-Tocopherol	Vitamin
Ramipril	Altace	Antihypertensive
Nifedipine	Adalat	Calcium Channel Blocker
Drospirenone; Ethinyl Estradiol	Ocella	Contraceptive
Hydrochlorothiazide; Valsartan	Diovan	Antihypertensive
Pioglitazone Hydrochloride	Pioglitazone	Antidiabetic
Famotidine	Pepcid	Antacid/Antiulcer
Methylprednisolone	Solu-Medrol	Corticosteroid
Clindamycin	Cleocin	Antibiotic
Risperidone	Risperdal	Antipsychotic
Rivaroxaban	Rivaroxaban	Anticoagulant
Hydroxychloroquine Sulfate	Plaquenil Sulfate	Antirheumatic
Aripiprazole	Abilify	Antipsychotic
Mometasone	Nasonex	Corticosteroid
Sumatriptan	Imitrex	Migraine Treatment
Dextroamphetamine; Dextroamphetamine Saccharate; Amphetamine; Amphetamine Aspartate	Adderall	Stimulant
Lansoprazole	Prevacid	Antiulcer
Baclofen	Lioresal	Muscle relaxant

Mirtazapine	Remeron	Antidepressant
Promethazine Hydrochloride	Phenergan	Antihistamine
Nitroglycerin	Nitrostat	Antianginal
Digoxin	Lanoxin	Anti-arrhythmia
Albuterol Sulfate; Ipratropium Bromide	Duoneb	Respiratory
Prednisolone	Prelone	Corticosteroid
Hydrocortisone	Cortef	Corticosteroid
Verapamil Hydrochloride	Calan	Calcium Channel Blocker
Ropinirole Hydrochloride	Requip	Anti-parkinson
Carisoprodol	Soma	Muscle Relaxant
Glyburide	Diabeta	Antidiabetic
Nebivolol Hydrochloride	Bystolic	Antihypertensive
Triamcinolone	Aristocort	Antifungal
Gemfibrozil	Lopid	Antihyperlipidemic
Omega-3-acid Ethyl Esters	Lovaza	Antihyperlipidemic
Budesonide	Pulmicort	Corticosteroid
Brimonidine Tartrate	Alphagan-P	Antiglaucoma
Doxazosin Mesylate	Carduran	Antihypertensive
Metformin Hydrochloride; Sitagliptin Phosphate	Janumet	Antidiabetic
Phenytoin	Dilantin	Antiepileptic
Solifenacin Succinate	Vesicare	Antimuscarinic
Calcium	Calcium-D	Mineral
Levofloxacin	Levaquin	Antibiotic
Canagliflozin	Invokana	Antidiabetic
Irbesartan	Avapro	Antihypertensive
Polyethylene Glycol	Miralax	Laxative
Acyclovir	Zovirax	Antiviral
Methocarbamol	Robaxin	Muscle Relaxant

Terazosin	Hytrin	Antihypertensive
Estrogens, Conjugated	Premarin	Hormone
Meclizine Hydrochloride	Bonine	Antiemetic
Mesalamine	Pentasa	Antiulcer
Testosterone	Andriol	Hormone
Desogestrel; Ethinyl Estradiol	Apri	Contraceptive
Lithium	Lithane	Antimanic
Temazepam	Restoril	Anti-anxiety
Memantine Hydrochloride	Namenda	Alzheimer
Oxcarbazepine	Trileptal	Antiepileptic
Metronidazole	Flagyl	Antibiotic
Valacyclovir	Valtrex	Antiviral
Magnesium	Uro-Mag	Vitamin
Nitrofurantoin	Macrobid	Antibiotic
Benzonatate	Tessalon	Antitussive
Liraglutide	Victoza	Antidiabetic
Guanfacine	Tenex	Antihypertensive
Sodium	Ocu-Disal	Electrolyte
Apixaban	Eliquis	Anticoagulant
Olmesartan Medoxomil	Benicar	Antihypertensive
Pramipexole Dihydrochloride	Mirapex	Anti-parkinson
Thyroid	Synthroid	Hormone
Adalimumab	Humira	Antirheumatic
Dicyclomine Hydrochloride	Bentyl	Anticholinergics
Anastrozole	Arimidex	Anticancer
Timolol	Timoptic	Antiglaucoma
Chlorthalidone	Thalitone	Antihypertensive
Lidocaine	Xylocaine	Analgesic
Phentermine	Fastin	Weight Reduction

Amiodarone Hydrochloride	Cordarone	Antiarrhythmic
Atomoxetine Hydrochloride	Strattera	ADHD
Ethinyl Estradiol; Etonogestrel	NuvaRing	Contraceptive
Fluconazole	Diflucan	Antifungal
Clobetasol Propionate	Clobex	Anti-itch, Steroid

Appendix B: Commonly Refrigerated Drugs

Generic Name	Brand Name
Actimmune	interferon gamma-1B
Amoxil	amoxicillin
Apidra	insulin glulisine
Augmentin	amoxicillin and clavulanic acid
Avonex	interferon beta-1a
Benzamycin	erythromycin and benzoyl peroxide
Betaseron	interferon beta 1B
Byetta	exenatide
Caverject	alprostadil
Ceclor	cefaclor
Ceftin	cefuroxime axetil
Cefzil	cefprozil
Cipro	ciprofloxacin
Combipatch	estradiol and norethindrone
DDAVP	desmopressin
Duac	clindamycin and benzoyl peroxide
Duricef	cefadroxil
Emcyt	estramustine phosphate
Enbrel	etanercept
Epogen	epoetin alfa
Foradil	formoterol
Forteo	teriparatide
Humalog	insulin aspart
Humira	adalimumab

Humulin N	NPH insulin
Humulin R	regular insulin
Iletin	insulin
Infergen	interferon alfacon-1
Kaletra	lopinavir and ritonavir
Keflex	cephalexin
Kineret	anakinra
Lantus	insulin glargine
Levemir	insulin detemir
Leukeran	chlorambucil
Miacalcin	calcitonin
Neulasta	pegfilgrastim
Neupogen	filgrastim
Novolin N	NPH insulin
Novolin R	regular insulin
Novolog	insulin lispro
NuvaRing	etonogestrel and ethinyl estradiol vaginal ring
Phenergan suppository	promethazine
Procrit	epoetin alfa
Rapamune	sirolimus
Rebetron	interferon alfa-2b and ribavirin
Suprax	cefixime
Tamiflu	oseltamivir
Thyrolar	liotrix
V-Cillin K	penicillin V potassium
Veetids	penicillin V
Vibramycin	doxycycline
Victoza	liraglutide
Viroptic	trifluridine

Xalatan	latanoprost
Zithromax	azithromycin

Appendix C: Vitamins

Common Name	Alternate Name
Vitamin A	Retinol
Vitamin B1	Thiamine
Vitamin B2	Riboflavin
Vitamin B3	Niacin
Vitamin B5	Pantothenic Acid
Vitamin B7	Biotin
Vitamin B9	Folate
Vitamin C	Ascorbic Acid
Vitamin D	Calciferol
Vitamin E	Alpha-tocopherol
Vitamin K	Phylloquinone

Bibliography

Morton Publishing Company. The Pharmacy Technician 6th Edition. Colorado, 2016.

Gilleon, Robbyn. PTCB Exam Study Guide 2017-2018. Copyright 2017.

Test Prep Books. PTCB Exam Study Guide. Copyright 2017.

Koborsi-Tadros, Sacha. PTCE. New York, 2016.

Kane SP. The Top 200 of 2018, ClinCalc DrugStats Database, Version 18.0. ClinCalc: http://clincalc.com/DrugStats/Top200Drugs.aspx. Updated February 3, 2018. Accessed June 3, 2018.

Made in the USA
Lexington, KY
30 September 2019